S0-ASI-342

Praise for *Hack*

"*Hack* is the best kind of ride: tough, sharp, determined, direct, fast as a death wish and every bit as heart-stopping."
—Koren Zailckas, author of *Smashed*

"[Melissa Plaut's] voice is perfect for these taxi tales: blunt, vernacular, laced with expletives, and utterly without pretense. For the ride she gives us—alternately mundane and hair-raising, hope-inspiring and horrible—she deserves a big tip."
—*The Providence Journal*

"A colorful guide to eking out a living in one of New York's hardest professions." —*New York*

"[Plaut's] likeable yet smart-aleck tone keeps *Hack* engaging and breezy. . . . Hack offers an invaluable front-seat view of the job's horrors." —*Time Out New York*

"You'll be transported to a world probably quite unlike your own. A world you may think of the next time you're figuring out how much to tip that cabbie." —*The Virginian-Pilot*

"Forget the Peace Corps—Melissa Plaut will tell you that cab driving truly is the hardest job you'll ever love. *Hack* is an honest and intrepid account of life in the front seat. Use a ten-dollar bill to bookmark your copy. When you're done reading, you'll use it to tip your next cab driver. Oh yes, you will."
—Wendy McClure, author of *I'm Not the New Me*

"When was the last time you shook your head in wonder? If it's been too long, read Melissa Plaut's brave, lurid, and completely improbable tale of life behind the wheel. You'll look at cabbies differently. You'll look at the world differently. *Hack* rekindles a sense of adventure we seem to have lost along the way." —David Goodwillie, author of *Seemed Like a Good Idea at the Time*

"This entertaining read highlights colorful characters as it reveals clever insights into the workings of a big city and the struggle to make a life." —*Body + Soul*

"*Hack* is the beat of the asphalt moving fast under our feet as we speed with Plaut through the city labyrinth on an always strange and new adventure." —Doug Aitken, artist

"This fast, funny behind-the-scenes tour of taxi driving in New York takes fascinating detours through issues of sex, class, and finding your life's purpose. Melissa Plaut is the Anthony Bourdain of cabbies." —Janice Erlbaum, author of *Girlbomb: A Halfway Homeless Memoir*

"*Hack* is an intimate portrait of New York City from within one of her most popular landmarks: the taxicab. Step inside; each page will ferry you through a hundred human stories about the stress of living in-between. From this carousel of urban life, Melissa Plaut opens the door to a new perspective on a misunderstood profession, and tells a redeeming story about the spirit of adventure that can be kindled within each of us— whoever we are, and wherever we are going."
—Travis Hugh Culley, author of *The Immortal Class: Bike Messengers and the Cult of Human Power*

HACK

HA

CK

How I Stopped Worrying About What to Do with
My Life and Started Driving a Yellow Cab

MELISSA PLAUT

VILLARD (V) NEW YORK

While all of the incidents in this book are true, some of the
names and personal characteristics of the individuals
involved have been changed. Any resulting resemblance
to persons living or dead is entirely coincidental
and unintentional.

2008 Villard Books Trade Paperback Edition

Published in the United States by Villard Books, an imprint of
The Random House Publishing Group, a division of
Random House, Inc., New York.

VILLARD and "V" CIRCLED Design are registered trademarks
of Random House, Inc.

Originally published in hardcover in the United States by
Villard Books, an imprint of The Random House Publishing
Group, a division of Random House, Inc., in 2007.

Library of Congress Cataloging-in-Publication Data
Plaut, Melissa.
Hack: how I stopped worrying about what to do with my life
and started driving a yellow cab / Melissa Plaut.
p. cm.
ISBN 978-0-8129-7739-4
1. Women taxicab drivers—New York (State)—New York—
Biography.   2. City and town life—New York (State)—New
York.   3. New York (N.Y.)—Social life and customs.
4. Taxicabs—New York (State)—New York.   I. Title.
II. Title: How I stopped worrying about what to do with
my life and started driving a yellow cab.
HD8039.T162U66   2007
388.4'13214092—dc22   2007019036
[B]

Printed in the United States of America

www.villard.com

2 4 6 8 9 7 5 3 1

Photographs by Melissa Plaut

Maps by Daniel Robert Lynch

Book design by Carol Malcolm Russo

To cabbies on the streets everywhere
but especially the New York hacks

And also
to
Ariel Schrag

Hack (hăk)

Function: *noun*

Etymology: short for *hackney*

1. a horse hired for riding or driving.
2. an old or worn-out horse used in service.
3. a coach or carriage kept for hire; hackney.
4. one who performs unpleasant or distasteful tasks for money.
5. a writer who does routine or commercial work, primarily for money.
6. *Informal*.
    a. a taxicab.
    b. a cab driver.

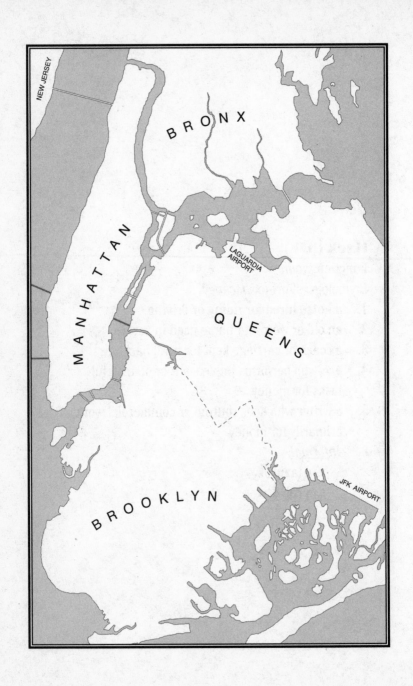

NEW JERSEY

BRONX

MANHATTAN

LAGUARDIA
AIRPORT

QUEENS

BROOKLYN

JFK AIRPORT

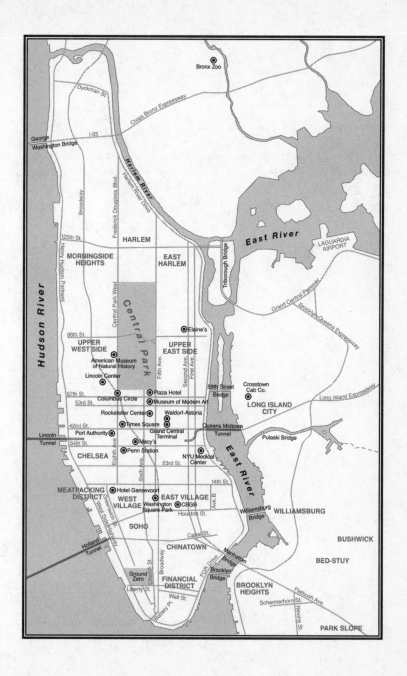

Bronx Zoo

Dyckman St.

Cross Bronx Expressway

I-95

George Washington Bridge

Broadway

Harlem River

Harlem River Drive

Frederick Douglass Blvd.

Henry Hudson Parkway

125th St.

HARLEM

East River

Triborough Bridge

LAGUARDIA AIRPORT

MORNINGSIDE HEIGHTS

EAST HARLEM

Central Park West

Central Park

Grand Central Parkway

Brooklyn-Queens Expressway

Hudson River

86th St.

Elaine's

UPPER WEST SIDE

American Museum of Natural History

Lincoln Center

UPPER EAST SIDE

Fifth Ave.

Second Ave.

First Ave.

57th St.

53rd St.

Columbus Circle

Plaza Hotel

Museum of Modern Art

59th Street Bridge

Crosstown Cab Co.

LONG ISLAND CITY

Long Island Expressway

Rockefeller Center

Waldorf-Astoria

42nd St.

Port Authority

Times Square

Grand Central Terminal

Queens Midtown Tunnel

Lincoln Tunnel

34th St.

Macy's

Penn Station

East River

Pulaski Bridge

CHELSEA

Eighth Ave.

Sixth Ave.

NYU Medical Center

23rd St.

14th St.

MEATPACKING DISTRICT

Hotel Gansevoort

WEST VILLAGE

EAST VILLAGE

Ave. B

WILLIAMSBURG

Washington Square Park

CBGB

Houston St.

Williamsburg Bridge

BUSHWICK

SOHO

Canal St.

Holland Tunnel

CHINATOWN

Manhattan Bridge

BED-STUY

Broadway

Church St.

Ground Zero

FINANCIAL DISTRICT

FDR Drive

Brooklyn Bridge

BROOKLYN HEIGHTS

Flatbush Ave.

Liberty St.

Wall St.

Battery Pl.

Schermerhorn St.

Nevins St.

PARK SLOPE

HACK

CHAPTER 1

I was an hour into my shift when I picked them up. Two guys in their early twenties got in at Canal and Broadway wanting to go to the tow pound in Brooklyn Heights to pick up their car. It was 5:00 P.M. and I knew traffic would be bad, but I didn't really have a choice. When they flagged me down, one of them held the back door open as he waited for the other to get a slice of pizza in the store. I started the meter but was already annoyed. It's a shitty way to begin any ride when they hold you hostage like that.

It was only when they got settled in the backseat that I realized they had been drinking. They were loopy and happy, but maybe a little too relaxed.

"Holy shit, look! It's a chick!"

"What?" the other one answered.

"Look! Our cab driver's a woman!"

"Oh, weird." They both gaped at me for a second, absorbing. Then, "Hey, can we smoke pot in here?"

I said no.

"Can we smoke a cigarette in here?"

Again, no.

I've never really understood why people want to smoke cigarettes so badly when they're in a cab. It's not like they're gonna be in there for *hours* or anything. Most likely they'll be in the cab for about ten minutes, maybe a half hour if there's traffic. And at the end of the ride they'll be able to smoke.

In the cab, however, it's illegal. Not like I'm some stickler for the law or anything, but I'm not gonna risk a $200 ticket, plus points on my license, for some shithead who can't stall his impulses until he gets out of my cab. The only reason to let people smoke is because you hope they'll show their appreciation by giving a bigger tip. But the few times I've allowed it, it just wasn't worth it. So what? They gave me an extra two dollars? Big deal. It totally didn't make up for the stress I experienced the entire time they were smoking. Plus, the smell lingers in the back, and when you get upper-crust antismoking Park Avenue types back there after that, you're screwed. They get upset and pretend to cough, and leave an even shittier tip than the shitty tip they'd already planned on leaving. It's just not worth it.

Of course, *I* smoke in the cab. But only under special circumstances. Like when I'm alone on my way back from far out in the boroughs or something, and I know the NYPD and the Taxi and Limousine Commission (TLC) cops won't see me, nor will they give a shit if they do. They really only care about stuff like that in Manhattan. And my reasoning is, since I'm stuck in the cab for twelve hours a night, I'm entitled to a smoke every now and then.

Anyway, we were sitting in traffic on the Brooklyn Bridge, and I heard that signature sound of beer cans cracking open. I called back to them, "Are you guys drinking beer back there?"

A guilty "No" reached my ears.

"No, seriously, are you? I heard the cans open and if you spill anything, you'll be putting me out of business for the night. And if the cops see us, I'll get a huge ticket. Please, just don't spiii it, okay?" At that point, it was the most I could ask for since I couldn't really kick them out on the Brooklyn Bridge.

Actually, I probably could've if I really wanted to. Paul the crazy Romanian dispatcher once told me a story about kicking a passenger out on the side of the Long Island Expressway. They were on their way to JFK airport and the passenger got mad because there was traffic, so he did what many other irrational assholic passengers have done—he blamed it on the driver. He started saying, "I'm not gonna pay for this. You're running up the meter. This is preposterous." But all Paul was doing was sitting in traffic, trying to get to JFK as fast as possible.

Some people seem to think that going slow and sitting in traffic is good for a cabbie since the meter is running. This couldn't have been more wrong back when Paul had his run-in, or during my first two years behind the wheel. The meter ran when the taxi was idling, yes, but it clicked off at a much slower pace than it would have if the cab had been moving. Traffic had an inverse relationship to our income, and we would essentially be losing money for the amount of time we were stuck sitting still. It was called "waiting time," but it should have been called "wasting time," since back then the rate for it hadn't been raised since 1990.

In December 2006, the TLC finally agreed to an increase,

doubling the waiting rate in order to almost catch up with the normal wage. But before this change took place, the meter used to tick off forty cents for every two minutes sitting still or in slow-moving traffic, which translated into $12 an hour. This was nothing compared to the forty cents we would get for every fifth of a mile driven while the cab was moving, which, if you were lucky—and fast—could bring in between $30 and $40 an hour.

The worst thing about the pre–December 2006 waiting rate was that it didn't even come close to what we needed to cover our regular shift expenses. Each twelve-hour shift, cabbies pay what's called a "lease fee" to take the cab, which is between $111 and $132, depending on which night you're working. This is the money we have to make back, plus our gas expenses, in order to break even, and that takes up the first four or five hours of the shift—sometimes more, sometimes less. After that, everything we earn is ours to keep, but the stress of starting out at around $160 in the hole sucks. Before the TLC increased the waiting rate, if I sat still with the meter on for the full twelve hours of my shift, I would've ended up *owing* money to the garage at the end of the night.

So Paul kicked the guy out of the cab, luggage and all, right there on the shoulder of the highway in the middle of nowhere Queens.

But I wasn't gonna do that, as much as I wanted to. These guys were assholes, but they were nice assholes. I mean, they weren't *trying* to be assholes. They started getting rowdy in the backseat, punching each other and play fighting, calling each other dickhead and cocksucker and bitch. Which was all fine, except the cab was shaking from the motion and I was afraid their beers were gonna spill, so I started throwing out empty threats. "If you guys don't chill the fuck out, I *will* kick you out right here. Calm down, okay?" If they forced me to, I would do it, but I really didn't want to.

When they heard this, they started back in on the woman thing. "Hey," one said, "I totally respect women. I think it's cool that you're a cab driver." The other, perhaps the brighter of the two, said, "If you respect women so much, why do you feel the need to say that every time you talk to a woman? Don't you see the problem with that?" Then to me he said, "Don't mind him. He's drunk, but he means well."

It's true I am sort of an anomaly. Out of the forty thousand licensed cab drivers in New York City, about two hundred are women, making up less than 1 percent of the cabbie population. It's no wonder people make such a big deal when they see me.

When we finally got off the Brooklyn Bridge, I had to look at the directions they'd given me to find the tow pound. At one point, I ended up in the wrong lane, a left-turn-only lane that led onto the Brooklyn-Queens Expressway. I didn't want that. We were at a red light and a minivan was on my right, so I put my right blinker on and tried to get the driver's attention so that maybe he would let me over. Turns out he wanted to make the left from his lane, the straight-only lane, and didn't see my signal, because when I pulled out in front of him, he stopped short and honked his horn at me. The guys in the back were like, "Oh shit, that guy almost hit you!" I said, "Yeah, I guess we were both sort of wrong there."

As I continued driving toward the waterfront, looking at the directions, I realized the minivan had abandoned his intended left turn and had started following me. Not only that, he was weaving in and out of the oncoming traffic lane, trying to get next to me. He kept racing up, getting next to me, and then hanging back when a car would come against him. But he kept doing it, and when he'd get beside me, he'd then swerve toward me from my left side, as if he was trying to run me off the road. I'm guessing he was mad.

My whole body went on red alert and I gripped the wheel hard with both hands, trying to keep the cab under control.

This guy was making me a little more than nervous. He wasn't backing down, wouldn't just let it go, and I wasn't sure what to do, didn't know what he was capable of. The guys in the backseat starting freaking out and yelling at him, but I had already learned that this kind of thing only encourages psycho drivers.

I heard their window open and I turned and said sharply, "DO NOT talk to him. Do not taunt him or encourage him. Do not engage with him at all or it will get worse for all of us. Okay? Please just put your window back up. Don't even look at him, okay?" They listened obediently and I heard the window go back up. If there was one thing I'd already learned in my short time as a cab driver, it was DO NOT ENGAGE. There will be thousands upon thousands of angry drivers on the streets, and whether they're righteous or not doesn't really matter, but the situation always gets worse if you enter into the verbal fight they're trying to start. All it does is get your blood boiling and your adrenaline racing. Besides, though it usually pisses them off even more if you just ignore them, it also gives you the upper hand.

I have to admit, there was a part of me that sometimes got off on the fight, but I'd learned I needed to preserve my energy if I wanted to make it through an entire shift.

As I made a left turn on Front Street, the guy turned with me, still on the wrong side of the street. My fear was building and I thought maybe I shouldn't go straight to the tow pound, which is in a relatively deserted area. Instead, maybe I should find the nearest police precinct and just park there until he got tired of wanting to kill me.

I went slow and he swerved in and out, behind me, then next to me, and even tried to stop short in front of me from time to time. I still wouldn't look at him. I refused to make eye contact and I continued pretending like he wasn't there. If he wanted to kill me, I wasn't going to give him the satisfaction of cursing me out first.

My passengers, however, had no problem looking at him, and finally, when he was next to us again, they yelled, "OH SHIT! HE'S A COP! Look over there, he's holding a badge!" I looked over and, sure enough, the guy was holding up a black leather wallet with a metal shield attached. I honestly didn't know if this made the situation better or worse. Worse, I think, since now he could kill me and get away with it if he wanted to. It's one thing to be almost run off the road by a road-raging psycho minivan driver, but when that driver is also an off-duty cop, there's something just so much more horrible about it. It's like he has a *right* to fuck with you, and you have no defense. If you fought back somehow, it wouldn't be considered self-defense, it'd be considered a crime.

Still, when I saw the badge, I slowed down. It's not like he was gonna give up anytime soon anyway, so I figured, let's just get this over with. If he wants to kill me, so be it. I was already fried from the whole ride.

I opened my window a little as he pulled up next to me, and he just started screaming, "You fucking bitch. You piece of shit whore. What the fuck is wrong with you? You almost hit me back there. You stupid fucking cunt." He went on like this for a minute, and I just replied, "I thought you saw my turn signal. I didn't mean to cut you off, I thought you saw me. Sorry." But there was no defending myself against his onslaught of *whore*s and *cunt*s and *bitche*s and *suck-my-dick*s. Very becoming behavior for one of New York's "Finest." Looking back now, I wish I had gotten his badge number. But I just sat there and absorbed his insults until he finally got his fill of abusing me and peeled out and away.

We were near the tow pound, but I didn't move for a minute. I felt like I had been punched. My heart was racing from all the fear added to the emotional beating I had just taken, and I was upset by my inability to defend myself. The guys in the back got serious. One of them said, "Look, I think we're close now. We can just walk from here. Don't worry about it." I could tell they felt bad for me.

I said, "No, I'll take you. It's no big deal." I just wanted to get them there and get them out, but I didn't want them to get out right there, like that. It didn't seem right, and felt even more like a defeat if I couldn't complete the ride. Still, I couldn't get rid of them soon enough, even though the rest of the way, they were being very sweet and nice, saying, "That guy was a lunatic. I can't believe he was a cop. That was so fucked up. Are you okay?" I nodded yes, I'm fine, thank you. I just needed a minute to put my head back together.

When we pulled into the tow pound, the fare was $11.90. They got out and stood by my window and continued trying to comfort me. I just said, "Please, it's fine. Can you just pay me? I gotta get back to the city." They shoved two $20 bills at me and said, "Keep it. And don't worry about that guy—he was probably a loser in high school."

I pulled away and carefully made my way back to Manhattan. Back in traffic on the Brooklyn Bridge, I lit a hard-earned cigarette and smoked.

On my very first day as a cab driver, a man stuck his hand in the open passenger-side window, made it into a gun shape, and said, "Gimme all your money." Then he pulled it back out and walked away laughing. My passenger thought I knew the guy, but I didn't.

Also on that first day, I saw a cabbie get punched in the face. There was a minor collision between a van and a cab, one having sideswiped the other, but who knows whose fault it was. Still, the cabbie always gets the blame. Both vehicles were stopped in the middle of the street and the two drivers stepped out of their cars. As I was passing through the intersection behind them, the van driver went up and punched the cabbie hard. The cabbie tried to block the punch, but it was too late, and he went down. I had a passenger in the back, and there was really nothing I could do anyway, so I drove on without stopping.

The plan when I got into this was to live life without regrets. To not settle for anything. To not get stuck behind a desk with a job I hated just because it paid well. In terms of life choices, I believed I'd rather regret something I *did* do than something I didn't do.

And this was what I had signed on for. I had to get used to it. I was scared and nervous and clueless that first day, but it was everything I wanted. My only regret so far was that I hadn't hit the gas and torn that motherfucker's gun-shaped hand off while he was sticking it in my window. But this was only the first test of my patience, and for the next two years, I alternated between an almost Zen-like mind-set and hair-trigger anger. I was trying to find some livable balance between my temper and a sense of calm, but instead of getting better with experience, it only got worse.

I got my hack license on my twenty-ninth birthday, September 1, 2004. I had spent the previous month, along with my last $400, going through the licensing process. When passengers ask, and they do all the time, why and how I became a cab driver, I know they're expecting some great story, whether it be some hard-luck bit or something about how cab-driving was passed down to me through the generations. That, or they think I'm a student romantically working my way through school. I feel confident that my tips would be exponentially larger if I let them believe any of these things, but unfortunately, the truth is much more boring.

The real story is that I grew up in Rockland County, New York, a suburb an hour's drive north of Manhattan. My parents both grew up in the city, but they moved my sister and me to the suburbs when I was one year old. They divorced when I was nine and both remarried within the next five years. They worked in the New York City public school system and commuted across the George Washington Bridge every day to their respective jobs in the South Bronx and Harlem. My mother was a speech pathologist, helping special-ed kids overcome their stutters and lisps. After twenty years in Harlem, my father moved on to become the principal at one of the city's most progressive public schools on the Upper West Side.

Their jobs were difficult, and all through my childhood, my parents told me to "never become a teacher." Of course, when I started driving a cab, they changed their tune. My father would send me newspaper clippings about how to apply for the New York City Teaching Fellowship, and my mother was eventually banned from suggesting other jobs, *any* job other than cab driver, every single time we spoke on the phone. Both are now happily retired.

I went away to college, first to the University at Buffalo, then transferring to the University of New Mexico in Albuquerque because it was cheap and off the East Coast. Unable to rest there and be satisfied, I spent my senior year abroad as an exchange student in Norwich, England.

I returned to New York after graduation and held a series of random jobs through the whole "Internet boom." After every company I worked for ultimately folded, I took a crappy corporate office job as a copywriter at a small ad agency down on Broad Street by the stock exchange, and I hated every second of it. But, despite the overwhelming dullness of the job, it was comfortable and easy and the money wasn't bad. I couldn't bring myself to quit, much as I wanted to.

When I graduated from college, I promised myself three things: (1) Never sell out; (2) Never settle; and (3) Never work in advertising. Actually, these three are all the same thing, but

I was twenty-two and I felt strongly about it. By twenty-six, I had done all three. I settled into a comfortable but shitty job as a sellout writer in a shitty advertising company. I had failed my younger, more idealistic self. So when they laid me off three years later, I didn't cry.

Instead, I collected my unemployment benefits until they ran out, and wasted a few months just aimlessly screwing around, hanging out, and not getting much done by way of my *life*. It was only when the money was almost gone that I decided I needed to figure out what was next. And that was the thing. I realized that up until that moment, I'd been trying to figure out what I wanted to be when I grew up, what sort of career I could get away with, and everything I had done so far was something I'd just fallen into by pure chance and luck. The jobs were nothing I felt passionate, or even particularly good, about. I needed a way to make money, and I guess I wanted some sort of security, but I didn't really care for any of the jobs I had done. I probably could've successfully continued on in the advertising industry, but I would've been committing to doing something I hated.

My best friend, Allie, always knew what she wanted to do with her life. She'd been drawing comics since she was a kid, and self-published her first book when she was a sophomore in high school. Since then, she has experienced a small degree of success with her later books, which were picked up by a legitimate comics publisher.

Early in our friendship, we spent a lot of time trying to figure out what my "thing" was. Her thing was comics, and she was really good at it. I desperately wanted a thing of my own to give me some sense of purpose and meaning, but up until then, I had never found it. We would sit around and try to come up with ideas.

When I was a kid, I never had an answer for what I wanted to be when I grew up, so I just copied my older sister, who knew since the age of four that she wanted to be a doctor. I co-opted her dream, and it annoyed her, but I didn't hang on to it for long. She eventually *did* become a doctor, while I scattered myself in a million different half-assed directions.

In elementary school, I wanted to be "the Fonz." That was about as close to a career decision as I had gotten to by then. By junior high, I had decided I wanted to become a rock star. I took guitar lessons and learned every Metallica and Iron Maiden song possible, until I realized just how bad I was.

Throughout high school, I was obsessed with the Mole People, who lived in the New York City subway system, and I wanted to join them. I was also interested in monkeys, and had fantasies about going to study them in Africa somewhere, but I didn't pursue it because of my intense phobia of bugs.

In college, I took human rights courses, and spent my time focusing on homelessness, visiting shelters and trying to come up with alternative housing options for people on the streets. I also grew interested in ancient history and mythology and wanted to go exploring around Iraq, since it was where the fertile crescent had been and, supposedly, where the last few remains of the Garden of Eden were. I saved up money so I could travel, but instead of Iraq, I went to Europe and Morocco and tried to see what the world was like outside my little self-obsessed bubble.

Drugs were another big interest of mine, and I spent a good couple of years doing them. But eventually they stopped bringing me any sort of remote happiness, so I abandoned that pursuit too.

When Allie and I became friends, I did the same thing to her that I'd done to my sister. I copied. I developed romantic fantasies of myself as some sort of artist, but since I couldn't draw, I decided maybe photography would be my thing. I took darkroom courses at the New School and SVA as part of their adult education programs, but I was never that good at it, and the hobby just sort of petered out after a while.

Then I thought my talent might lie in video, so I bought a digital video camera. Allie and I would sit around my bedroom inventing little skits and playing them out for the camera, which we propped up on top of the TV so we could watch ourselves while we acted. I taught myself how to use a bootlegged copy of Final Cut Pro, and spent hours editing our plays into two-minute spots that no one but us thought were funny.

After that, I switched over to thinking about math. That was something I had actually always been good at, so I bought a bunch of old calculus textbooks at the Salvation Army and sat at my kitchen table working out equations and reteaching myself everything I had forgotten from high school. But still, it was more of a hobby than anything else. I *still* couldn't find my goddamn *thing*.

My problem was an existential one. Each thing seemed as good as the next. It was just an arbitrary decision that, in the end, had no meaning anyway, so why bother? I wasn't driven by some intense passion like my sister, and didn't have any innate talent like Allie. I wanted so badly to believe in the idea of a true calling, something a person could spend their days feeling passionate about and engaged by, but it just didn't exist for me. Unlike Allie, I was driven more by cynicism and restlessness, and it had no outlet. I was stuck in a pit of indecision and there was no place for me to put all this energy, so I ended up spending a lot of time being mad at everybody.

Eventually I got the horrible advertising job, and a part of me had just given up. My soul was being sucked out on a daily basis in the corporate world, and I stopped caring. I had resigned myself to a passionless life in a boring office doing something I hated. It was the antithesis of a "thing." My life seemed more meaningless and purposeless than ever.

After I got laid off, I decided to stop. I was no longer going to try to figure out this "rest of my life" bullshit. Instead, it was all about what was *next*. It was as simple as that. I was gonna treat life as the adventure I wanted it to be. I wanted to try to get as many experiences as possible under my belt before I was dead, and I didn't want to die in some office somewhere in the Financial District. Just working there was a death in itself.

I had always thought about driving a cab, just thought it'd be interesting and different, a good way to make money while getting to see the city in a totally new and intimate way. In fact, I'd considered trying it out the *last* time I was unemployed, five years earlier. But it always just seemed like a fleeting whim, a funny idea, something I would never actually do.

When I told Allie I was planning on getting my hack license, she didn't think I would really follow through with it. I had come up with so many un-followed-through-with ideas up until then, she thought this was just another caprice, another fantasy, another example of me trying to figure out what to do with my life without ever actually doing anything about it. But I had reached my breaking point. I felt an urgent need to waste no more time. Since I couldn't decide on *one* thing, I would do everything, or as much as I could get away with in one lifetime. And I had to start somewhere. I went down to the main TLC office in Long Island City, Queens, and got the application.

CHAPTER 2

It's not the easiest thing in the world to get a hack license. And since the Taxi and Limousine Commission is a bureaucratic city agency, they make sure you not only pay what seems like a ton of money to get licensed, but that you also jump through hoops to get it. There are a lot of steps in the process, and they decided somewhere along the way that you have to do everything in a certain precise order.

First, I had to upgrade my regular driver's license from a Class D to a Class E, which required simply going down to the DMV and giving them $40. Then I sat through a six-hour defensive-driving course before getting my medical exam, which consisted of going to some doctor in Queens who took my blood pressure and shined a flashlight into my eyes. After the two full minutes spent with her, I handed over the $15 fee, she signed the form, and I was sent off with a clean bill of health.

After that I had to get a form notarized that stated I did not owe any child support. Everyone has to do this, even if, like me, you don't have children. There were some other forms that needed filling out, and once all these steps were taken care of, I went back down to the TLC offices and waited in a hellishly long line to turn in my application.

When you're sitting in that waiting room, even if it's only for two or three hours, it feels like a week. Every few minutes, a new red-dotted number lights up on the LED boards around the room, and the soft little ding that accompanies it makes everyone look up from their newspapers and books on the off-chance it's their number being called. The men grow beards waiting there. And the women—well, there weren't any. I was the only woman there, not counting the ones who worked behind the bullet-resistant windows.

When my number finally came up, the lady behind the counter combed through my application like a detective, trying to find problems with it. At one point, she looked at my driver's license and said, "You've had a change of appearance. You need to get your picture retaken and come back."

I was dumbstruck. "What?"

She took a deep breath and spoke very slowly, as if this was the most tedious question in the whole wide world and I was a small, annoying child just learning to speak English. I got the feeling she treated every new applicant this way. "You've *had* a *change* of *appearance*. We can't put your application through if you look different from the picture on your license."

A change of appearance? The picture on my license was maybe two years old, but the only differences were that I had gained a few pounds and gotten a haircut or two. I couldn't believe what she was saying. I had waited there for three fucking hours and now she was gonna send me away with nothing because my hair was four inches shorter than it was on my license?

I said, "My hair grows really fast. By the time I get a new picture, it'll already be a lot longer. Isn't there anything you can do?"

She gave out a big obnoxious huff and called over a supervisor for a second opinion. Luckily the supervisor was much more reasonable. She looked at the picture, looked at me, looked back at the picture, and said, "She's fine. Put her through." The original lady sucked her teeth and gave a little smirk, as if she thought the supervisor was being too easy on me, as she stamped my forms and took my money.

I handed over the $120 for the licensing fee, plus another $70 for the fingerprinting, all in separate money orders made out to different parts of the bureaucracy. I was given a slip and told to wait in a separate area to get fingerprinted.

When my name was finally called, a man sprayed down the greasy glass reader with Windex and carefully rolled each of my fingertips over it until all ten were done. Then he had me sit for my mug shot.

The wall behind my head had a big oil stain on it and I positioned my head away from it so it wouldn't touch. This was the picture that was to go on my license, so I tried to smile and look easy and smart and worthy of big tips. He showed me the first shot and I hated it. I made him take it two more times before I finally gave up on looking anything but weird and dorky.

After all this, I was given a little blue slip and directed to the building around the corner to take the drug test. And when that was done, I proceeded farther down the street to enroll in taxi school. This was the second-to-last requirement for licensing. And taxi school was mainly to prepare everyone for the taxi test. If you passed the taxi test, and your application wasn't denied for some bullshit bureaucratic reason, you were an official New York City cab driver.

"Manhattan has the most perfect address system in the world because of him." The teacher pointed at my fellow student named Hamid. "Why? Arabic numerals, babba, that's why."

At 9:00 in the morning I was sitting in my first class at the Taxi and For-Hire-Vehicle Driver Institute, located within LaGuardia Community College. It, of course, was in Long Island City, Queens, the center of the taxi universe. The intensive three-day course was designed to help potential drivers pass the taxi test, and the teacher, a man named Frank Roberts, was already filling us with important information, more than half of which we would forget immediately.

Not only was I the only female in the class of about fifteen men, but I was the only U.S.-born citizen, other than Frank. When I walked in, everyone looked at me like I was in the wrong room, which was understandable. They must have assumed I was one of the thousands of regular college students filling the halls around us, and that I had accidentally stumbled into the one room in the building that contained a bunch of older immigrant men, men who were there not in pursuit of a bachelor's degree but rather to get a hack license. I just sat down and opened my map to pass the time until class started. No one said anything. They just drank their coffees and tried not to stare.

When Frank finally breezed in, the first thing he did was take each person's name and write it down in a list on the chalkboard. It included names like Phillipe, Brutus, Hamid, Javed, Benny, Bablu, Isaac, Ahmed, and, naturally, Melissa.

Frank was a middle-aged white man dressed in a denim button-down shirt, an American flag tie, and khaki pants. He'd been driving a cab for twenty-four years and teaching this class for nine. He'd been a medic in Vietnam and had traveled all over the globe. He appeared to know not only every single detail a person could possibly know about New York, but amazing facts about every other country in the world as well.

Frank stood at the front of the classroom, next to the broken taximeter and the mock cab that was set up out of schoolroom chairs, and began to teach. He spoke to each student in his own language, and made jokes that under other circumstances would have sounded painfully racist but, because of his breadth of knowledge and high level of cultural sensitivity, instead came off as funny and endearing. It took less than five minutes for us all to be completely in awe of him.

He informed us that there were 31 water crossings, 138 landmarks, 6,400 miles of streets, and 11,107 street names in New York City. And we were going to have to learn as much of them as we could for the test. He also told us that the reason cabs were yellow was because the cones of the human eye see that color first.

When speaking to us as a group, he usually addressed us all as either "babba" or "driver." But when singling us out, he gave us each a nickname, which he chose spontaneously and which was for the most part based on each student's ethnicity. Phillipe was Haitian Prince, the guy from Africa was Motherland, Javed became Shah Javed, Hamid was known as Sultan Hamid. There was also Russian Bear, but that got complicated the next day when another Russian guy joined the class, so they were divided into Big Russian Bear and Little Russian Bear. Ahmed became Brother Ahmed, someone was deemed Papa Tiger, another guy was called Grandpa, and me, I got three nicknames. I guess he couldn't decide what I should be, so I was alternately called Young Sweetheart, Princess, and Our Star.

A month or so later, I met a twenty-five-year-old white guy named Mike who had been driving a cab for nearly three years and who'd also had Frank Roberts as his teacher. He was in taxi school just after the war in Afghanistan started, and one of his classmates turned out to be Afghani. This man's nickname, of course, was Taliban. Mike's, on the other hand, was American Eagle.

The reason Frank could get away with this was because he knew almost as much about each of these guys' home countries as they did. It was clear that he'd been everywhere and had done just about everything. And when he told us to take out our pens, he would say the word "pen" in Arabic, Creole, Russian, and any other language a student in the class might speak.

In addition to the geography of New York City and the TLC rules, we were also to learn how to use a map. Frank said, "Okay, driver, would you go with me to box N-25 in your street atlas?" And when the class took too long to find the right page, he said, "I can walk there faster! Come on, boys!"

When we finally got there, he continued, "Find Grand Army Plaza. No, not the one in Manhattan. We're in Queens now. *Kfeens!* I am using a Russian Jewish accent. *Kfeens!* Okay, babba, found it? But wait! There's yet *another* Grand Army Plaza! Can you find it on your map? I'll give you a hint: It's in Brooklyn."

Frank slowly pieced the city together for us borough by borough, and, in between the geography lessons, he educated us about the taxi industry.

"Ahmed, can we make you a rich man?" When Ahmed agreed, he continued. "Okay, good. Ahmed owns a fleet. He has three hundred yellow cabs. He's a *tycoon*. Now, in order to legally pick up street hails, every cab must have a medallion. Each medallion is worth about three hundred thousand dollars—Hong Kong dollars? No. *Oosa*, babba, *oosa*," he said, pronouncing "USA" as if it were a word.

"Ahmed, think big, you wealthy Islamic businessman!" Frank said, and then he turned to the rest of us. "If you multiply three hundred by two, that's six hundred shifts a day that this rich man, Ahmed, is making money off of *you,* driver." And he waved his hand over the rest of the class. "Multiply that by three hundred sixty-five days, and you get the idea. Like I said, he's a *tycoon.*" Then he did a jaunty little dance and said, "In Africa, we have a saying: All men have the right to dance, said the elephants among the chickens."

We were all completely confused. Frank clearly existed on a totally different plane than the rest of us. He was a rambling savant, New York incarnate, the star of his very own theater of the absurd, but he made sense in his own crazy way. It just took us all a while to catch up to him. I wondered if this was the sort of sage wisdom and genius insanity that accumulates after a certain number of years behind the wheel of a yellow cab. Or if it was just who Frank was. A part of me hoped it was a product of the job, because, whatever it was, I wanted a piece of it.

"Now, what *you* have to do, after you get your cab from Ahmed the tycoon, is get in that car and get on that island," Frank continued, punching his finger into Manhattan on the wall map. "Why, babba? Because it's the center of the center of the world. And why is that?" At this point, he took a small wad of money from his pocket, brought it to his nose, and smelled it deeply. "Money, babba. That's why."

Frank taught quickly. There wasn't a lot of time to prepare us for the test, and if you failed it twice, you had to start the entire application process over again. He turned to Javed. "Okay, babba, it snowed in Bangladesh, do we agree?" When Javed didn't answer, Frank said, "Ah! Javed's just shy. He's a typical gangster. Javed, you like chicken tikka, is that fair to assume?" Javed smiled and nodded, not knowing where this was going.

Frank said, "Okay, let's drive to Bombay and get some chicken tikka!" And after a dramatic little pause, he leaned close to Javed and said in a loud whisper, "Can we drive to

Bombay, babba? Nooo. That'd be very expensive, and hard to do, I would think."

He straightened himself up and continued, "Since we can't drive our cab to Bombay, *India,* let's go to Bombay *Street* on Staten Island. Find it on your maps now! Go, go, go!"

After the fluttery sound of frantically turned pages subsided, Frank said, "If you can't find it, it should be in box C-13. But, what do we have here? Javed the Shah is whining that the chicken tikka isn't spicy enough, so we're going over to Calcutta Street to look for something better. Can you find it on your maps? Come on, driver, I'm in a hurry! Who taught you how to drive, anyway? I'm swimming there faster than you! Now, babba, let's go to Brooklyn. Find box R-10. I'm now using my Punjabi roll: Rrrrajasthan-10 . . ."

After lunch that first day, when Frank came back with what looked like a chocolate stain on his denim shirt, we learned that the meter clicks over forty cents for every fifth of a mile driven, coming to about two bucks per mile. If you go anywhere beyond the city limits, you can charge a flat rate or you can double the meter, making out of town jobs the most lucrative. I was surprised to find out that no one is required to wear a seat belt in a New York City yellow cab, not even the driver. I'm not sure what the reasons for that are because I couldn't stop Frank in time to ask.

On our breaks, the classroom would erupt into heated political debates about immigration and green cards and all sorts of other things. I felt ignorant and didn't have much to contribute to these conversations, but I listened intently and learned a lot.

These guys were not born cab drivers. Many of them had been lawyers, engineers, or architects, or they'd held some other equally respectable white-collar position in their home countries, but their advanced degrees and experience weren't recognized by American employers, and they were stuck in "the land of opportunity" with no real opportunities other than cab-driving. They had fallen from an elevated standing to what in New York is seen as the bottom of the barrel.

I, on the other hand, was coming from a very different place, and I felt a little weird about it. I could've had white-collar opportunities if I wanted them, but I simply wasn't pursuing them. Not like I was getting any job offers or anything, but I could've sent out a tidy little résumé and pursued that career in advertising if I'd really wanted to. And even though, by that point, I was totally broke, I was still coming from a place of privilege, and I felt a certain amount of guilt about it when confronted with my classmates' individual situations.

They didn't hold it against me. In fact, over the next few days, they accepted me as one of their own, and I ultimately became a focal point for the entire class. This was mainly due to me being female as well as my seemingly good grasp on New York geography. And I suspect this is why Frank began calling me Our Star.

On the second day, Frank instructed us on how to prepare for fare-beaters. He said, "Okay, babba. A beautiful woman gets into your cab. She leans forward to show you her two best friends and says, 'Driver, take me to Thirteenth and Third. And will you wait for me? I have to run in and get the money.' Of course, when you arrive, she says, 'I'll be right back, handsome. Will you just wait for me here?' "

Frank continued, "So you wait. And after a while, you start wondering if she's okay and you go in the store to look for her. Do you think she's still there, babba? Of course she's not! She's gone! There's a back door, and you've been beat!"

The main lesson, according to Frank, was, "Don't trust anyone, babba, because they're all con artists and criminals in this city."

He also instructed us to never, ever chase fare-beaters—a commonsense rule I was one day to break—and if someone sticks a gun to your head or a knife to your neck, just hand over the money. The one piece of self-defense advice he did offer was to honk the horn if someone tries to run. This might at least get the attention of someone who could potentially help you.

A month after taxi school, Mike the American Eagle gave me another piece of advice. He said, "Always wear your seat belt. That way, if someone tries to rob you in the cab, you can just hit the gas and slam into the closest car or pole. When the robber's head smacks into the partition, you can get away and call the cops. I mean, what's the difference? It's not like you own that cab anyway. Who cares if it gets busted up?"

This was exactly the kind of stuff my mom was so worried about. It was all she could think of when I told her I was going to be a cab driver, and she pushed very hard against the idea. I tried to calm her down by telling her that this kind of stuff didn't happen anymore, which wasn't entirely true, I suppose. It did happen, but a lot less than she, in her Jewish-mother way, imagined. The possibility of getting robbed definitely scared me, but I was also sort of stupidly thrilled at the prospect of danger. I didn't really take it seriously at the time, just never imagined it actually ever happening.

By the end of the third day at taxi school, our heads were crammed with information. Frank had not only prepared us for the test, but he had also tried to prepare us for the often-bitter reality of cab-driving. The basic list of advice he left us with was: get on the streets early, don't get lost, don't get stuck in traffic, don't get a ticket, and don't have an accident. Easy enough.

Beyond that, after three full days of taxi school, there was not much more he could do for us. The rest we would have to figure out for ourselves.

I went home and studied for the test. I was nervous about it, not sure if I would remember all the things I might be asked. We were given practice tests and I forced Allie to quiz me over and over until she was bored to death. What's the best route to Shea Stadium from city hall? Where is the Sheraton Manhattan Hotel located? Which Central Park transverse is nearest to the children's zoo? Which diagonal thoroughfare connects Bensonhurst with Brownsville? It went on and on.

Friday morning I met most of my classmates outside the room where the test was to be held. The door was locked and the monitors hadn't shown up yet, so we all sat around comparing notes. Everyone was jittery and we quizzed one another and tried to clear up all the last details we were still confused about. Frank wasn't coming, so we had only one another to rely on.

"Where the hell is the Cooper-Hewitt museum? I couldn't find it anywhere in the book!"

"Does anyone know where the entrance to the Macombs Dam Bridge is on the Bronx side?"

The hallway was filled with a frantic roar of questions and jumbled answers involving street names and intersections, parks and hospitals, bridges and tunnels. We thumbed through our notes and work sheets, our maps and handbooks, in a classic last-minute-before-the-test cram-fest.

We were to be monitored by two members of the TLC staff. When they arrived, everyone quieted down and filed into the classroom. They explained the rules with cold voices. Already we understood that these people were to be our enemies once we passed the test. Already they despised us, and we weren't even cab drivers yet.

The first part of the test consisted of an English proficiency exam. There was a machine that played an audio recording of a man and woman repeating street names and destinations, such as "Fifty-seventh Street and First Avenue," in steady monotones. Then the man or woman in the recording would instruct us to look at our books, where we'd see a question that said "Where does the man want to go?"

Once that was done, we moved on to the rest of the exam, the true test of our knowledge, where all the geography and rules questions were asked. I thought I did okay.

After the test was over, we all hung around outside, comparing our answers to the questions we were unsure of, saying goodbye, and wishing one another luck. I never saw any of my classmates again.

On Tuesday morning the following week, I called the school to see if they had gotten our test results back. They had. I got a ninety-eight. I was to receive my license in the mail within the next few weeks. I was now officially a New York hack.

CHAPTER 3

There are about fifty taxi fleets in New York City where you can lease a cab by the shift. The deal is, you pay to take the cab for twelve hours, the standard length of a shift, and the rates vary depending on which day or night of the week it is. Days are cheaper than nights, weekdays are cheaper than weekends. You're also responsible for your own gas. So, all told, I was going to have to pay out somewhere between $130 and $180 just to get started.

Since I didn't know how to choose between garages, one of the administrators at taxi school recommended I check out

Crosstown Cab Company, a medium-size fleet in Long Island City, of all places. They had about 150 cabs and had been in business for decades. I was told they would be nice to me there.

When I showed up, I was "broken in" by David, a dark-skinned, dark-haired, good-looking Jewish guy in his forties. He was a civil engineer who had become a partner in the garage, his father's business, and he basically ran the operation on a day-to-day level. He was married and had twin sons, and he seemed pretty straitlaced, but his appearance was deceptive. A month later, when I wore an old Yo La Tengo T-shirt to work (they're an indie rock band from Hoboken), David not only knew of them, but also owned all their CDs. I realized we actually had something in common, and he might not be as buttoned-up as he looked. Our up-till-then polite rapport got much warmer and turned more toward the side of friendship. After that, David was my biggest ally at the garage, always giving me a good car, getting me out of the lot early, and generally helping me whenever I needed it.

That kind of stuff could happen at Crosstown. David was the third generation in a line of taxi driver/owners. His grandfather was a cabbie a million years ago and started up the fleet. He passed the business on to his son, David's father, who also drove for a while after coming back from WWII. It wasn't a corporate, management-run garage, which was how most of the big fleets operated. Rather, at this garage, the owners worked on-site, dispatching drivers as well as just generally interacting with them, and it gave the place more of a mom-and-pop feel.

Of course, it wasn't always perfect. David's father was a seventy-six-year-old five-foot-tall man named Lenny, and he was prone to outbursts. Lenny dispatched drivers on weekday mornings, starting at 4:00 A.M., a cranky time for most people— but cranky was Lenny's baseline, and it only got worse as the day progressed. In fact, Lenny was rumored to be the real-life prototype for the Louie De Palma character from the TV show *Taxi,* the show's creators having discovered him while scouting garages back in the seventies, and I could totally see the similarity. He was crotchety, ill-tempered, foulmouthed, and sometimes just plain crazy.

If a driver had the great misfortune of running into Lenny after having had even a minor collision, Lenny would practically burst out of his tiny hunched frame to unload a vast range of curses and invectives. Often the unlucky driver would tower over him and quietly take the abuse, though there was always one or two guys who dared to fight back, which, of course, only made things worse. Some guys hated Lenny so much they would quit the garage and move on to a different fleet, where things were handled in a more corporate—and professional—manner. But this didn't happen too often because David and the third partner in the business, an Iranian guy named Eddie, were around to balance Lenny out, soothing us with their cool heads and kind compassion, and that was usually enough to keep most drivers on board. It was much like any other dysfunctional family or workplace.

On the weekends, things were a little different, with Paul the crazy Romanian dispatching the night drivers. A large guy in his mid-forties or so, he was a younger, Eastern European version of Lenny, though he did occasionally exhibit a sensitive side that Lenny seemed to lack. And, on the other end of the night shift, a young, good-looking guy from Algeria named Omar worked as cashier, settling up the lease fees with the drivers bringing their cabs back during the early-morning hours.

Monday through Friday, a guy named Warren cashiered for the day drivers while Paul came in and cashiered at night. All of these guys were ex-cabbies, now preferring to work their twelve-hour shifts in "the cage" rather than spend them out on the streets.

That first day, David showed me to a taxi parked in the lot and put me in the driver's seat of this "stretch" (for more passenger leg room) Ford Crown Victoria, the standard model in the industry. It was my first time in the driver's seat of a yellow cab.

David got in next to me and gave me the rundown.

"Did they show you how to use the meter in school?"

"No. The one they had was broken."

"Ahh, you're lucky you came to us. Most garages in this town would just put you in a cab, point to Manhattan, and send you off."

He showed me how to work the meter, explaining that the roof light—the light on top of the cab with the medallion number on it—goes off when the meter is turned on, so that people on the street can know that the cab has been hired. When the meter is turned off, the roof light goes back on to indicate the cab is vacant.

He let me turn it on and off a few times to make sure I understood. I was a little embarrassed to be so clueless, but I worked up the nerve to ask, "So what's the deal with tipping and the meter and stuff? How much money goes to me?"

David seemed genuinely surprised. "They didn't tell you that in school either? You keep everything, the metered fare plus the tip, as long as you make enough to pay your lease fee plus gas and tolls. After that, the rest is yours. You'll make more money once you get the hang of it, but a good way to gauge it is, you should be taking home at least twenty-five dollars more than the garage makes for your shift."

"Okay. . . . So what can I expect in terms of tips? I mean, like, what's normal?"

David was patient with my total lack of knowledge and answered, "Most people tip at least a dollar, but if it's more than eight or ten bucks, you should probably get about fifteen or twenty percent, like a waitress in a restaurant. But don't get upset if someone doesn't tip you. There are plenty of jerks out there who won't. But if you're a good driver, you'll do just fine, especially being a young white girl who speaks English. They'll love you."

After this, he moved on to the business of the trip sheet. The reasons for filling out a trip sheet have never been clear to me. You put in the time each trip started, where you picked up, where you dropped off, the time you dropped off, the number of passengers, and the total cost of the trip.

Some people claim the trip sheet has something to do with tracking down criminals, and there was an urban legend about the FBI tailing a suspect from Kennedy airport. The story went that the guy got into a yellow cab and the feds lost him in traffic on the highway back to Manhattan. Having written down the cab's medallion number—the number that is all over the cab, on the sides, the license plate, and the roof light—they traced the cab back to its garage the next day, looked at the destination written on the trip sheet, and learned where their suspect had been dropped off.

Most cabbies, however, believe the trip sheet is there to provide the TLC with yet another reason to ticket them. Didn't put your signature on the trip sheet? That's a $25 ticket. Didn't write "Off-duty" when you stopped to go to the bathroom? Another twenty-five bucks. If the number of trips on your meter doesn't match up to the number of trips on your trip sheet, that's yet *another* ticket. No cabbie I ever met had seen a trip sheet be used by the TLC or any other official for anything other than writing tickets and bringing the city just a little more revenue.

Next, David gave me a crash course in garage procedures and etiquette. If working the day shift, he explained, I should show up at 4:00 A.M., get dispatched a cab, and go to work, arriving back no more than twelve hours later. For the night shift, I should arrive around 2:00 or 3:00 P.M., give the dispatcher my hack license, and wait around for my name to be called. As cabs rolled in from the day shift, the dispatcher called out names over the loudspeaker, sending them out according to the order of licenses in the stack. Sometimes you could get sent out right away, and sometimes you could wait there for a few hours, getting frustrated and losing any remaining desire to work.

When I came back at the end of my shift, I'd need to fill up the gas tank and tip the mechanics a buck or two for the service. If I brought the cab back late, as in more than twelve hours after I got it, I'd be charged $10 an hour for each hour over.

In terms of tipping people out, I was confused. Frank Roberts had told us that we should tip dispatchers five or ten dollars as a sort of bribe so they would jump us in line and get us out early, giving us a head start on the shift. But David explained that this didn't fly at Crosstown. Over the years, they'd had too many dispatchers taking advantage of drivers, so they put an official end to the practice and now it was strictly first come, first served. The only people who should be tipped were the mechanics and the cashiers.

There was so much new information to remember, I was afraid I would forget it all instantly. As he was wrapping up the last details, David looked me up and down and said, "You gotta be tough to do this job."

I got a little defensive and replied, "I'm tougher than I look. I'll be fine."

"I never said you weren't tough. I'm just warning you—it's not easy."

We got out of the cab and I was handed off to Lenny, who took me into the office upstairs and gave me a two-hour "prep course." This included hints on where to go during which times of day and how to make the best money, some of which I eventually discovered to be true, and some—not so much. It was the first time I met him and one of the only times over the next two years that I'd see him in a calm, almost *good* mood.

"Work the right side of the avenues, that's where the best fares are. If you're working the day shift, work uptown in the mornings. Try to stay on the Upper East Side—that's where all the people live who go to work in midtown or Wall Street. Nights, do the opposite 'cause they're all going home. Late Friday or Saturday nights, get over to the bars in Alphabet City or the West Village. Learn where the clubs are. And don't refuse any passengers unless they're drunk or disorderly. If you refuse a fare for any other reason, you can bet they'll call 311 and complain about it."

He was referring to the city's main information and complaint line, instituted by Mayor Michael Bloomberg, and it seemed that New Yorkers were in love with it, especially if they had a complaint about a cab driver. If a complaint was filed against you, you had to go downtown to TLC court and sit in front of an administrative judge who could impose a hefty fine, put points on your license, and even suspend or revoke it if he or she felt the complaint merited such punishment. The worst part of this was that cabbies were generally considered guilty until proven innocent, and everyone in the taxi business thought of TLC court as a kangaroo court.

Lenny explained things in bullet-point form for a while as I studiously and nerdily tried to write it all down. Most of it was common sense, but I was nervous. He ended by saying, "It's a dirty job. When you go home after work, all you'll want to do is take a shower and wash the city off your skin." Then he gave me directions on how to get onto the 59th Street Bridge, both the upper and lower levels, and sent me back downstairs, telling me to come back tomorrow to get started.

When I walked into the waiting room the following morning, the first driver I met was a guy named Harvey as he was coming off the night shift. He was hard not to notice. Harvey was a portly sixty-something-year-old white man with a blond Afro, and he was dressed entirely in women's clothing.

His attire consisted of black stretch pocketless cotton pants pulled up over his midsection, a purple turtleneck, a floppy pink bell-shaped hat on his head, and white Keds on his feet. He also wore lipstick and nail polish.

When we introduced ourselves, Harvey looked at me with curiosity, intrigued by what the hell someone like me was doing there. I thought his getup was a good cabbie shtick, something to impress the tourists and amuse hardened New Yorkers.

I said, "So, do you dress like that for the tips or what?"

He gave a terse smile. "Something like that."

Cabbies used to do stuff like that all the time to get better tips. They would dress up funny, decorate the insides of their cabs, put up their head shots on the partition that divided the front and back of the car, have a repertoire of jokes they could tell for the duration of the ride, or even just play the role of the quintessential New York cabbie. I figured Harvey was doing something along these lines.

His Brooklyn accent was unmistakable, and his voice was deep and manly. He used to be a tour guide on the Gray Line double-deckers, but somehow was fired and had been driving a cab for too many years. He knew a lot about New York, and was also incredibly skilled at math, performing complicated equations in his head in just a few seconds. I found him to be a little obnoxious, though. He rolled his eyes at half the things I said and made me feel stupid, like I was a little know-nothing dilettante who wouldn't last a week as a cabbie. He spoke with a tone of utmost authority and was constantly contradicting everyone, David and Lenny included. I wasn't sure if I liked him.

There was another driver there who I also couldn't help but notice, but for very different reasons. His name was Ricky and he smelled like piss. To be fair, Ricky was an old man in his seventies and had diabetes. But still. As I discovered over time, Ricky would show up every day at the garage reeking, to the point where people were not able to sit near him in the waiting room.

He was an odd guy and, for whatever reason, was always wanting attention and help from me. I figured it was because he was lonely and I was one of only two women working out of that garage, and because I was at least ten years younger than almost everyone else there. When I first started, Ricky was always asking me to throw things in the garbage for him. I used to do it just to humor him because he was old and had some trouble moving around, but it eventually became so excessive, I told him he had to throw things away for himself.

Then he became obsessed with telling me over and over, every time he saw me, "You're gonna be here for thirty years." I don't know why he believed that, but I always hoped he was wrong.

His next phase was to repeatedly tell me I reminded him of his cat. When I asked him the cat's name, he answered, "Rhoda." The next day, he compared me to his cat again. I said, "Her name's Rhoda, right?" But he said, "No. Her name is Francie."

Though there were definite similarities, as evidenced by Lenny, this wasn't the garage of the sitcom *Taxi*. There didn't seem to be many moonlighters anymore, people working at something during the day and driving a cab at night to support their more creative endeavors. Of course, there were still a few—there was one middle-aged actor and one young photographer, but that was about it. Most of the cabbies there were full-timers like the Alex Rieger character on that show. Except that they were mostly all South Asian and with families to support, both in America and back home. They were career guys, just cabbies, working six or seven twelve-hour shifts a week to make ends meet.

I was never going to be a full-timer, I just didn't have the balls for it. At most, I only worked three or four shifts a week, if that, but it still racked up to between thirty-six and forty-eight hours on the job. I was also determined to not get sucked in forever and become a lifer, and this was a little easier for me because, unlike these guys, I didn't have anyone to support but me, my two cats, and maybe a little video game addiction. But that was about it. So I threw myself into the job full force, determined to be a "real" cabbie, despite my part-time status and despite the fact that I would never work as hard or as long at it as most of the other guys there.

Long Island City is one of the westernmost neighborhoods in Queens, located just across the East River from Manhattan. It was developed at some point as an alternative to congested midtown since it was right across the 59th Street Bridge, and some banks and financial companies tried to go along with the trend and settle there, but the idea never really took off as well as anticipated. The neighborhood was an unusual mix of vast industrial tracts, power plants, out-of-character apartment towers, glass-windowed office buildings, and taxi fleets. It was similar to Williamsburg, Brooklyn, in the sense that it was just on the other side of the river from Manhattan—which everyone who lives in the outer boroughs simply refers to as "the city"—and provided close proximity and cheaper apartments for people who couldn't afford Manhattan rents. Unlike Long Island City, however, Williamsburg eventually became wildly successful as the postcollegiate destination of choice for young artists and yuppies-in-the-making. I lived in a sixth-floor walk-up on the outskirts of Williamsburg, on the border of Bushwick, a drug-filled, largely Puerto Rican neighborhood that was only then starting to see the spillover of gentrification from Williamsburg proper.

I started out on the day shift, driving my 1989 piece-of-crap Buick over the Pulaski Bridge, which connects northern Brooklyn to Long Island City, and arriving at the garage at 4:00 A.M. It was an island of muted bustle and activity in an otherwise fast-asleep neighborhood. The only other movement in the area came from the bread trucks and the coffee carts that emerged from a warehouse down the block, and the last of the late-night drinkers closing down the go-go bar next door.

A few drivers were milling around the garage, reading the paper, washing their cabs, and getting themselves geared up for the day. I approached the dispatch window, where Lenny slid a trip sheet and a car key into the curved metallic slot underneath the Plexiglas, like you see in a bank or a token booth, and directed me to a cab out in the yard.

It was pitch-dark and there was a slight September chill in the air when I settled into the front seat, snapped my trip sheet into my brand-new clipboard, and tried to familiarize myself with the car itself. I tested the meter, making sure I remembered how it worked; slid the window open in the bullet-resistant partition that divides the front seat from the back; checked all the lights and signals; and adjusted my seat so that my feet were the perfect distance from the gas and brake pedals. I lingered a little longer than necessary, trying to make sure everything was in place, savoring the moment, and trying not to let all the feelings of expectation, excitement, and terror paralyze me. My heart was beating extra fast and everything around me seemed simultaneously immediate and unreal, but I put the car in reverse and backed up.

It was not quite morning yet when I pulled out of the lot, and I carefully made my way to the 59th Street Bridge and on into the city. As the skyline of Manhattan came into view on the bridge, I could hardly believe I was actually doing it. In that one quiet, intensely private moment alone in the cab, I felt the hugest rush of exhilaration I had ever experienced in my life up till then.

That first day, it took me two hours to get my first fare. She was a middle-aged Spanish waitress just coming off work from a diner on 14th Street and Avenue B in the East Village.

I was so nervous, mainly about going the wrong way, but she soothed me. "How long have you been doing this?"

I didn't want her to know how green I really was, so I lied. "About a month."

"Do you like it?"

"Um, yeah. It's okay so far."

She said, "I've actually been thinking about getting into it. Was it hard to get your license?"

I explained the process and encouraged her to try it, said we needed more women drivers on the streets to balance things out a little bit. I tried to act like I knew what I was talking about.

At the end of the trip, she said, "Here, I'm giving you everything I made in tips tonight," and handed me a total of $14 for a $10 fare. I couldn't thank her enough.

CHAPTER 4

Those first weeks, I found myself plagued with indecision. I was familiar enough with the streets and correct routes, but sometimes one route seemed just as good as another and I couldn't decide which way to take. This problem carried over from my normal everyday life, where I had difficulties in deciding such things as what to name my cats, what to major in at college, what to do with my friends when we went out at night, and slightly bigger things like what to do with my life. My thinking was, it didn't really matter what I did, it was all arbitrary, the same, and ultimately meaningless anyway. And this became a real obstacle for me in the cab since it had never been more important to be quick and decisive.

But other than having difficulty making route choices, my biggest problem in the cab at that time was my fear of getting lost. Every time a passenger entered the cab and told me their destination, I felt a rush of adrenaline and nervousness. I tried to plot the absolute best, most efficient routes, but sometimes I made mistakes, despite my best efforts.

The few times it happened, the mistakes were minor. Above 14th Street, Manhattan is laid out in a simple street grid, with avenues running north–south, and streets running east–west. The only avenue that defies this is Broadway, which runs the entire length of the city in a diagonal direction. With all this efficient urban planning, and allowing that you're not way downtown in the pre-street-grid Financial District or West Village, it's actually quite difficult to get lost in Manhattan.

Still, I found myself getting tripped up by little things. One late afternoon, a business-suited passenger wanted to go from midtown to 79th Street and Amsterdam on the Upper West Side. Easy enough, I thought, and I headed north on Sixth Avenue, west on Central Park South, and then north again on Central Park West, choosing that instead of the heavily congested Broadway. But when I got up to where the turn for 79th Street should have been, I realized my mistake. The Museum of Natural History was in my way, running along for four blocks between 77th and 81st. I had completely forgotten about it. It was a minor mistake, but it was a mistake no seasoned cabbie would ever have made.

I felt like a total idiot and was starting to stress out, working myself into a small frenzy, and with every pause in the guy's cell phone conversation, I worried that he was judging my route and getting annoyed with me. I boxed around the block back down to 79th, and when I dropped him off, I turned to him and tried to apologize. "I'm sorry we had to go around. I totally forgot about the museum. I'm kind of new."

He held the phone half off his ear and said, "Huh? Oh, yeah, it's fine." Turns out it was no big deal after all, he had barely been paying attention. He even gave me a decent tip in the end, which I certainly didn't expect, or even deserve, for that matter.

Still, I managed to make quite a good share of stupid little mistakes like that back in the beginning. And there were plenty of people who *were* paying very close attention, and who would get extremely aggravated, huffing and puffing and complaining from the backseat. And this, oftentimes, would be reflected in their tip, or lack of one, as the case might be. These people didn't care if I was new. They just wanted to get where they were going as fast as possible and had no interest in being my training coach. Those five extra blocks registered about forty cents on the meter, but I think a lot of people were more concerned about the extra time, and the annoyance of having a cabbie they couldn't trust to get them from A to B in an efficient manner. Usually, my five-borough street atlas was no help for these kinds of things, so I started making notes on the map when it didn't match the reality of the streets, in order to avoid making the same mistakes twice.

The first time I got really, truly confused about where I was, however, I wasn't alone at night in the big bad Bronx or anything like that. I wasn't even anywhere near Manhattan, for that matter. Rather, I was at Kennedy airport in Queens. I had just dropped off my passenger and, having made it there without any mistakes or mishaps, I decided to try to find the Central Taxi Hold lot.

At Kennedy airport, most people get off a plane, walk outside, and see a line of taxis waiting there. They might be directed to one by a dispatcher, get in, give their address, and never give the process a further thought. But for cab drivers, there's a whole ordeal that goes into picking up at JFK, and even at LaGuardia, for that matter.

Both airports have taxi "holding lots," where we are required to pull in and wait our turn behind all the cabs that pulled in before us. At Kennedy, it's one enormous lot that serves the entire airport and that, at full capacity, holds about five hundred cabs. It's a pretty awe-inspiring place and quite a sight to see when there are fifty rows of yellow Ford Crown Victorias all lined up like that, the planes landing practically on top of them.

When I dropped off my passenger, I left the terminal determined to try it out, even though Frank Roberts had told our class it was a waste of time to wait at the airports. He said, "Drop off and get back on that island, because *that's* where the money is, babba."

But it seemed like every cabbie had a different opinion. Some, like Frank, got rid of their passengers and raced back to the city as quickly as possible, while others religiously pulled into the taxi hold lot, no matter the capacity, considering it a nice little break while remaining on the job.

I decided to give it a try. The only problem was, I couldn't find it. Kennedy is a massive airport and its service roads, if you haven't spent much time on them, are utterly confusing. I pulled out of the terminal and spent the next thirty minutes driving in circles, moving deeper and deeper into the pit of the airport, but instead of the taxi lot, I found only cargo lots, rental car places, airplane hangars, gas stations, and hotels. I knew that the lot was supposed to be two miles from the terminals, but I couldn't find a single sign telling me which way to go.

The rest of the airport, away from the bustle of the terminals, was totally desolate. It was already after 8:00 P.M., and it seemed that much of the place had shut down for the night. Or if anything was still operating, it was happening behind closed doors or gates and not out where an inexperienced cabbie could stop and ask for directions. When I did finally find an open gas station, the attendant was no help at all.

Circling around, there were a few times when I risked accidentally entering forbidden areas—security-restricted cargo-loading hangars and lots—but was able to stop and turn around in time to avoid getting into any real trouble. As I was making one of these hasty U-turns, I imagined an armed guard in camouflage, high-laced boots, and dark sunglasses, with a big automatic rifle, sitting up in a watchtower somewhere, keeping an eye on me. He was chewing on a toothpick and was clearly something straight out of Rambo or some other Green Beret–type movie. Precious top secret military cargo is being loaded and unloaded, and the guard up in his tower puts me in his crosshairs and a little red dot shows up on my forehead. At the last possible second, I pull a move straight out of Grand Theft Auto, my favorite video game, and swing a hard 180-degree turn, evading the sniper bullet just in time, and racing to the safety of the taxi lot in high-speed fashion.

Unfortunately, I couldn't press pause in this reality. I was losing time, and I lost even more of it checking and rechecking my atlas. The general layout of the airport was shown in the front pages, but that still gave me no indication of where I needed to go. It was like the taxi lot was a secret club that only the worthy got to be initiated into. Or maybe, like some scenarios in Grand Theft Auto, you needed to complete a certain amount of missions to unlock the board. I considered giving up and just heading back to the city empty, but I had already wasted so much time and invested so much energy into this, it seemed like doing that would be a total defeat. I renewed my determination to find that goddamn lot, even if it ruined my entire night.

I drove around the sprawling complex at least three more times before, totally frustrated and confused, I found my way back to one of the terminals and asked a traffic cop for directions. He pointed toward a certain exit ramp and said, "Just follow the empty cabs." I spotted a few of them driving away from the terminal with a palpable sense of urgency, so I took his advice, falling in behind them and trying to keep up.

Within five minutes, I was inside the lot. I almost couldn't believe it. I had begun to wonder whether or not it even existed at all. When I finally pulled in and drove through a structure that appeared to be some kind of tollbooth, I just copied the cab ahead of me until he parked, taking my place in line with a few hundred other yellow cabs.

The Central Taxi Hold lot at Kennedy airport is a lot like the United Nations, with representatives of nearly every country in attendance. Of course, the majority are from Southeast Asia. And they're all men. The anomaly of a female cab driver had not previously been as apparent as it became when I pulled in there.

If you're unlucky, the wait there can last up to three or four hours. On the other hand, if you pull in at just the right time, when the airport is busy and planes are coming in loaded with passengers, the wait can be as short as twenty minutes. The normal waiting time, though, is usually between one and two hours. To pass the time, a lot of the guys there play backgammon, dominoes, and will even hold a game of cricket if the weather's right. But mostly everyone just stands around or piles into a buddy's cab and shoots the shit. There's also a coffee shop inside the lot that is a hive of activity and passionate conversation, and there's a flat concrete area behind it where, at certain hours, the devout Muslims lay down mats, take off their shoes, and pray. In the winter, the praying takes place inside.

That evening, the lot was about half-full. I saw men entering and exiting the men's room outside the coffee shop, but when I went to the women's room, it was locked. An African man standing nearby informed me that I needed to get the key from inside, and on my way into the building, I passed through a crowd of Haitian men having a spirited political debate. As I moved past them, they all fell silent and stared at me.

Once inside, I had to squeeze through an unruly line of guys buying tea and sandwiches, cigarettes and juices, donuts and bagels, to get to the front, where I was able to trade in my car key for the bathroom key. This was attached to a twelve-inch metal pole. I had to pee, but I had to go through such a sucky process in order to be able to do that, while at the same time, all the men could just come and go and piss as they pleased.

The Greek men working the counter were nice to me, at least. I guess they'd realized somewhere along the way that if they left the women's room unlocked, the men would just use that bathroom too, which probably wasn't the best idea, for legal as well as hygienic reasons.

I grabbed the key and beelined it back to the women's room. When I finally got in, after a few tries with the difficult lock, I appreciated its relative cleanliness and privacy. I also liked knowing that none of the sleazier men could just barge in on me.

When I finished, I again had to battle the line to return the key, but this time I felt a lot less urgency about it, so I tried to take it in stride. I bought a donut and went back to my cab, still trailing stares after me wherever I went.

The guy parked in front of me did a double take when he saw me unlock my cab, and a few minutes later, he came over and started up a conversation. His name was Nicholas and he was from Pakistan.

"How long have you been doing this?" he asked.

I was embarrassed to be so new, but he seemed nice and genuinely interested. He wasn't leering or looking at me like *What are you doing here?* so I told him the truth.

"Almost three weeks."

"Ah!" he replied, as if he remembered his first weeks all too well. "It'll get easier. You'll be fine, don't worry."

I said, "So what happens now?"

He replied, "We sit and we wait."

"How long you been driving?"

"Two years. It's terrible. I'm really an engineer, but when I came to this country, no one would hire me without an American degree even though I'd been practicing for thirteen years."

We stood there chatting for a while, and he explained the ins and outs of waiting at the airport, until his phone rang. Headset already in his ear, he answered and spoke to someone in Urdu.

I leaned against the hood of my cab, listening to him talk while I smoked a cigarette.

When he finished up his conversation, I asked, "So do you, like, talk while you're driving the cab?"

"All the time."

"Who are you talking to, other drivers?"

He laughed. "Who else? There are about five of us who all conference together when we can."

"Do you talk about your passengers?"

He looked at me with pity, like I was maybe a little retarded, and said, "Yeesss. In fact, the whole way here, I was saying to them, 'This fucking guy, taking me to JFK in the middle of this crap traffic, the fucking asshole.' "

"You're lucky you speak another language. I wish I did, then I could bitch too."

After about forty-five minutes, the lane next to us was moving out and the cabs in our lane started their engines back up. When we started filing out, I followed Nicholas through the tollbooth, where each cabbie was given a ticket with a terminal number on it.

I had another moment of panic when I got my ticket with a

big number one on it, but Nicholas slowed down in front of me and stuck his hand out the window, holding up his index finger to show me he, too, was going to Terminal 1. I gave him a thumbs-up out my window and he waved for me to follow him. We went back out into the maze of airport byroads and onto the JFK Expressway, until we finally reached Terminal 1, which serves only international flights. We entered an area that said AUTHORIZED VEHICLES ONLY and got on another, much shorter taxi line, the line that the passengers see and wait near.

When Nicholas's passengers got settled in, he didn't leave right away. Instead, he waited until my passengers also got seated, then yelled out the window back to me, "Manhattan?"

When I nodded, he said, "Good. Me too. Follow me." He led me out of the airport and onto the Van Wyck Expressway, where I was finally able to relax a little, knowing that the way back was easy from there. However, when the traffic on the Van Wyck came to a standstill, Nicholas signaled for me to follow him again as he got into the exit lane and left the highway, most likely with the intent to take the less congested service road.

I was too scared to follow. It was my first time ever taking a passenger from JFK to the city and I finally knew where I was. I wanted to stick with the route I learned in taxi school, even though I knew there were other ways, ways that circumvented the traffic that, I soon discovered, practically *defined* the Van Wyck. But, that day, I didn't want to take any more chances.

I watched Nicholas get off the expressway while I stayed in the traffic, inching my way slowly but safely back to the city. When I dropped my passengers off at Tudor City, a small, historic neighborhood near the United Nations, they gave me an $11 tip on the $45 fare.

The next time I was at the airport, I got lost again looking for the lot, but this time it only took me twenty-five minutes to find it. That was the last time it ever happened. And, randomly, every few months after that, I would run into Nicholas on the streets, our cabs pulling up side by side at a light, each of us looking over, recognizing the other, and then smiling and waving with a laugh.

The only other thing I was really afraid of was the possibility of getting robbed or ripped off. The robbery thing was a relatively distant possibility, but fare-beaters were still around and going strong. I was aware of this, but it wasn't a reality to me just yet. Of course, it became one real quick, within my first week of driving, when I was still working the day shift.

I wasn't quite smart enough yet to recognize when a potential passenger might try to beat the fare. Or maybe I just wasn't discriminating enough. I wanted to be so even and fair and humane in my role as a cabbie that I was very idealistic about it. I wanted to act in a way that would allow me to live with myself and my conscience.

This unjaded approach had indeed worked out well for me already on one occasion. In that instance, I had just begun my shift at 4:00 A.M. When I came over the 59th Street Bridge, I was behind about ten other empty cabs also making their way into the city.

The ten split up at the bottom of the bridge, half going toward Second Avenue, and the other half heading toward First Avenue. It was morning, so I went for First Avenue as well, adhering to Lenny's advice to work uptown at that time of day.

On First, after about twenty barren blocks, I saw two black guys standing on the street with their arms up, trying to hail a cab. At that point five or six empty cabs were in front of me, but I watched with surprise as every single one of them slowed down, took a look at the two guys, and then sped off without stopping. By the time I got near them, I was almost scared, thinking maybe there was a reason all these cabs were passing these guys, maybe they knew something that I didn't.

When I got alongside them, my passenger-side window was open enough to hear one of them say, with a tone of despair and confusion in his voice, "Why are all these cabs passing me?"

I took a deep breath and stopped the cab. The guys got in and said, "Thanks for stopping." I congratulated myself on how noble and unprejudiced I was for picking them up. I was still worried, however, that they were going to direct me to some destination in the Bronx or deep Harlem, or some other "bad neighborhood" where I still didn't know my way around.

One of them said, "Ninety-third and Lexington, please." I exhaled and thought, *See, they're just going to the Upper East Side. They're not bad, nothing to be afraid of.*

I tried to make conversation. "How are you guys this morning? Where you coming from?"

"Just smoking weed and playing video games for *way* too long."

They joked around between themselves for the rest of the ride, and in that moment, I promised myself that *I* was going to be different, or at least different from all those other cab drivers, the ones who passed these guys because they were black. I would never pass anyone based on their skin color, because I knew I wouldn't be able to live with myself if I did. Sure, I wasn't perfect in terms of my prejudices—who is?—but I vowed not to act on them. I wanted to be good and right and decent and fair.

What struck me the most was that some of the cabbies who passed these guys were most likely Muslim or Sikh men from foreign countries, men who experience their own special form of racism in America. And yet, they *still* wouldn't pick up two black kids on First Avenue. It was a little depressing to think about.

I dropped the two guys off without incident. They paid the

fare, tipped, thanked me, and emerged from my cab thinking only about their beds.

However, trying to be open-minded didn't always pay off. Later that same week, I learned my first lesson in who I actually *should* be discriminating against. It was mid-afternoon on a Saturday when I picked up an unshaven shabby old white guy near Bellevue Hospital on the east side.

He had a cane and a green army overcoat, despite the warm weather, and he took forever to get seated in the cab. I tried to be patient and sympathetic—clearly he had some sort of physical ailment—but it literally took him about five full minutes to get in, and I was getting anxious.

When he finally got seated, he directed me to the Chelsea flea market on the west side. After a minute of silence and without any provocation, he started unfolding his story for me. "They just worked on my kidneys in the hospital there. That's why I'm on this cane."

I tried to be polite, saying, "Oh really? Well, it's good to see that you're okay."

"Yeah, I just got out. I wanted to stay one more night, but Medicaid wouldn't pay for it."

A red flag immediately went up in my mind. *Medicaid? What is a guy on Medicaid doing taking a cab*? Maybe he was just desperate for a ride and decided to splurge.

"Oh," I said, trying not to worry about it.

"And they wouldn't even arrange for my ride! Can you believe that?"

"Why wouldn't they give you an ambulette? Don't they usually do that kind of thing?"

"Nope. Medicaid won't pay for that either."

When we were about three avenue blocks from his destination, he said, "You know, honey, I don't have anything on me."

Refusing to understand right away what this meant, I said,

"Huh? What do you mean?" I tried to imagine maybe he was talking about drugs, or a gun, or anything other than money.

"I don't have any cash. You see, they just let me out of the hospital, and I'm sort of in between places right now, and . . ."

I felt myself get hot with anger. "What do you mean, you don't have any money? You're kidding, right? Don't tell me you got into this cab knowing you couldn't pay for it. I'm not doing this for charity, you know."

"Well, where I'm going is where my old boss is. He has a booth at the flea market. I can try to find him and see if he'll give me the money."

I didn't really know what to do. I thought, *Should I kick him out right here?* We were only three blocks away, and he *was* on a cane, though at that point I began to wonder if the cane was a prop and this was a scam. Fuck it. The damage was already done. I took him the three blocks.

At the corner, he said, "Just wait here. I can go find him and try to get the money." But I knew he wasn't about to hobble all around the flea market and back just to get the seven stupid dollars he owed me. And besides, even if he was sincere about it, at the rate he moved, it would've taken him an hour.

I said, "No. Forget it. Just get out."

I was bitter, but his reaction wasn't. "God bless you! God bless you! Oh, you've done a very nice thing!"

A few weeks after that, I made the mistake of picking up another old scraggly white guy, this time uptown, on 101st and First Avenue. He jumped in right as the person I was dropping off was getting out, so I didn't even have a chance to look at him first.

He directed me to 86th and Lex, not a far ride and in a decent neighborhood, so I was fine with it. Of course, when we got there, he didn't have the full fare. He only had three dollars and offered to go "meet his friend" and get the rest of the

money, but I knew this was another scam story—especially because, by that point, I had the definite impression that he was
going to buy drugs or do some other shady deal.

I thought, *Who the hell are these people who get into a cab
without having the money to pay for it?* I grabbed his three
shitty dollars and instructed him to get the fuck out of my cab
before I called the cops.

I'd had enough. When I drove away from him, I made a
promise to myself: No more fucked-up old white guys. I don't
give a shit if they're bleeding or crying or on their knees beg-
ging, if they're on a cane, crutches, or in a wheelchair. After not
getting the full fare twice in two weeks from these characters,
they had *earned* my discrimination, and I felt perfectly justified
enforcing it. From then on, this was the only potential passenger
I would purposefully pass by without stopping, not that there
were that many of them actually hailing me. Still, if they *did* hail
me, they weren't getting any favors from me, and that was that.

When I told the other drivers at the garage about it, they
weren't impressed. It happened all the time, unfortunately, and
they considered me lucky to have only lost a few bucks both
times. "Just let it go," they said. "Move on. There's no time to
worry about it. Just make it up with the next guy. Don't waste
even more time and money on it."

I had a hard time accepting it, but I knew they were right.
There was nothing I could do about it but make it worse.

After two weeks on the job, I switched over to the night shift.
During the days, there was too much traffic, too many cops
and rules, and, no matter how hard I tried, I simply could not
adjust my sleep schedule to wake up at 3:00 A.M.

Nights were better. I could easily stay up all night and sleep
all day. I would arrive at the garage anytime between 2:00 and

3:00 in the afternoon, stand around waiting for the day drivers to bring the cars in, and was usually out on the streets with my cab by 4:00. By 8:00 or 9:00 P.M., rush hour ended and traffic eased. There was also more money to be made at night, and more interesting people, and it wasn't nearly as scary as I'd originally thought it would be.

I also started to feel a little more comfortable in the cab. I already had the basic layout of the city tattooed inside my brain, and felt more confident, with barely any trace of that beginner's nervousness left. But I was still no expert. That level of knowledge takes many, many years behind the wheel, and even when I'd had two years on the streets, I still relied on my older cabbie friends for directions to remote locations in the outer boroughs, as well as all the other sage advice that they offered me so generously.

While I was still new, I was the nicest cab driver anyone had ever had. People actually told me that. In the back of my mind, I had a feeling it wouldn't last, but I tried not to acknowledge this reality. I would politely ask people if they wanted to hear the radio, and which station, and I would eagerly start conversations, happy to tell them about myself. I was just so excited to finally be doing this, to be meeting all these people, and to be learning the city in a way I had never even imagined was possible.

About a month into my adventure, I met an old-time driver who would become one of my closest cab-driving friends at the garage. He was an insanely tall, lanky, scruffy middle-aged guy wearing jeans and a plaid button-down shirt. When I walked in, he was standing at the Ms. Pac-Man machine trying to beat his own high score. I always thought it was funny, the very cab-specific symbolism of Ms. Pac-Man: a yellow disk speeds around a neon-lit grid eating white dots and getting chased by ghosts.

I watched him play for a few minutes, and when the GAME OVER screen appeared, he turned and introduced himself to me. His name was Daniel and he'd been driving a cab since 1979. He was incredibly nice to me, and when I told him I was a little drained from the job, he gently patted my shoulder and, in a comforting tone, said, "Don't worry, it'll get easier. I promise."

Daniel liked to work only on the Upper East Side. He was keyed into the area better than any global positioning system could ever be, and he tried his best to stay there for his entire shift. He also loved to get fares to the airports, and, over time, we held countless debates on whether or not it was worth it to sit in the taxi hold lots waiting for a fare back. Of all the cabbies I'd met so far, Daniel was definitely the sanest.

While we were waiting, Paul the crazy Romanian was dispatching. As the day drivers pulled in and gassed up, Paul would pick up the next license in the stack and call the driver's name over the loudspeaker. Each conversation at the garage was punctuated with interruptions like "Viktor the criminal, you're up" and "Morris the terrorist, get your ass over here," all spoken in a thick Romanian accent so that each consonant had a hard edge. The din of voices lulled for a second as everyone tilted their ears to make sure it wasn't their name being called. And the guy who *was* called peeled off from his conversation, picked up his license and trip sheet at the dispatcher's window, and went to work.

Day drivers were slowly trickling in, names were being called, and Daniel and I were standing around talking when Harvey showed up. This day he was wearing the same black stretch pants, the top of which produced a horizontal line that starkly divided his body into upper and lower portions, a pink turtleneck, pink nail polish, and red lipstick.

Daniel turned to him and said, with a good-natured chuckle, "Harvey, I don't understand. Your nail polish doesn't match your lipstick? Why not?" Harvey replied in his deep, almost frog-throated voice, "Ah, yes, but my nail polish matches my shirt, and my lipstick matches my blush. You clearly don't know anything about female attire, my friend."

Daniel said, "Well, you look beautiful!"

Harvey answered, "Thank you." Then he turned to me and said, "And how are you, my dear? You dying out there yet?"

"Pretty much," I said. Then, "No, I'm just tired. But I'm doing okay, I think."

Harvey settled into a teacherly tone, saying, "Well, you have to think of it this way: You're the captain and the passengers are just your cargo. Unfortunately, most people don't see us that way. They like to be the boss, and you their hireling."

He paused, and then said, "My advice? Get out of this while you still have your sanity. It's the worst job you'll ever do. To be frank, I'm surprised you've stuck it out for this long already."

This annoyed me, yet I was happy that I had proven him wrong. And I realized that, even though I didn't necessarily *like* Harvey, I found myself caring about what he thought of me. And *that* annoyed me the most.

I was about to offer him some non-reply, some type of, "Well, here I am" bullshit answer, when over the loudspeaker came "Daniel my boyfriend."

Daniel said, "That's me. Okay, guys, knock 'em dead out there."

To which Harvey replied, "I always try, but my aim is a little off these days."

The thing about driving a cab is that it's all so random. You never know who's going to jump in and you never know where you'll end up. The passengers are a mixed bag of characters and most things about the job are completely unpredictable. I had been noticing one pattern, though, where every now and then it seemed like there was a certain progression to the evening. It started with people going home from work or out to dinner and perhaps some other form of entertainment, such as a movie or a play. After that, they would have drinks, sometimes taking a cab from one bar to another. A few hours deeper into the night, they were drunk and acting a little stupid. And finally, later, they were very drunk, acting *very* stupid, and were barely able to make it home without passing out or puking in the back of the cab.

It wasn't like that every single night, but that was the basic formula, especially on weekends. A few months into my cab-driving career, I'd already had many nights that adhered to this structure perfectly.

One night early in my shift, I picked up a young, beautiful woman going to meet her date. It was around 7:00 P.M. and I picked her up on Park Avenue and 96th Street, near where the elevated Metro-North tracks duck underground on their way to Grand Central Terminal. The woman's brother had flagged me down so he could hold the cab for her while we waited for her to come downstairs. She was running late and was clearly feeling a little rushed.

I didn't want to be held there and was starting to get anxious, but when she finally jumped in, I relaxed as she said, "Thanks so much for waiting. And, don't worry, I'm a good tipper." I just sort of mumbled that it was okay as we hurried down Park. She went on, "Seriously. I know how it is. I dance for a living. . . . You know, like, I'm a stripper."

I said, "Oh really? Where?"

"You know the Hustler Club?"

"On Fifty-first and the West Side Highway?"

"That's the one. It's not too bad. But it's not the best either."

I was bringing her to a fancy restaurant in midtown, so I commented, "I take it you're not working tonight."

"No," she said, "I'm actually going on a date with some guy, and I *so* don't feel like wasting my time."

"So why are you going, then? Couldn't you just cancel?"

"Well, he's taking me to see *Wicked*. You know, the musical? And I really want to see it."

"That's not such a terrible thing."

"Yeah, and when he asked me to go, I tried to say no at first by telling him I didn't have anything to wear. So he went and bought me this dress. I want to keep it, and I want to see the play for free, so I'm just gonna go and get through the night and never see him again, hopefully."

From what I could see of it, it was indeed a nice dress.

"At least you're getting something out of it. That's more than you can say for most bad dates."

The meter was at $9.40 when we got to her corner. She handed me a twenty, told me to keep the change, and hopped out in her expensive dress.

I love strippers.

The post-dinner going-out-for-drinks phase of the night officially began a few hours later when I picked up two middle-aged white guys near Port Authority. They started asking the usual questions, about me being a female cab driver and whether or not I was Jewish, where I was from and how old I was, and so on.

After answering these questions for what already felt like the millionth time, I finally got to ask what they did for a living. One of them said, "I'd rather not say."

I said, "Okay . . . why not?"

He replied, "I'm Italian. Let's just leave it at that."

"Oh. I think I get it." I assumed this meant he was in the Mafia or something, but I wasn't totally convinced, thinking he might be testing my gullibility.

Then he said, "I adhere to a code of silence. We call it

omertà." At this point, I didn't really want to push it, just in case he wasn't kidding. The other guy just sat there silently.

They were making two stops. I dropped the Italian guy off at Elaine's, a famous restaurant and celebrity hangout on 88th and Second, where he was meeting people for more drinks. As he was exiting the cab, he insisted on paying the full fare over the objections of his friend, and then said to him, "All right, bye. I love you, asshole!"

When we pulled away, his friend said, "Now that he's gone, I can tell you what he really does: He's a Catholic priest." This was probably the actual truth, but frankly, the Italian mobster story was more fitting.

As the night wore on, the stupid drunks started pouring out onto the streets. Around 1:30 A.M. I was sitting in front of a bar on Spring and Hudson when all of a sudden some genius jumped onto the trunk of my cab and started bouncing up and down, being a perfect drunk dick. When I hopped out of the cab and started yelling at him, he bent over and said, "Look at my ball! Look at my ball!" pointing at his testicles and, for whatever reason, referring to them in the singular.

When he finally stopped, he and his friends came over to me and said, "Hey, you're not a terrorist. Why are you driving a cab?"

I said, "Are you fucking kidding me? What the hell are you doing? Don't you dare touch this cab again."

They seemed almost ashamed for a second and I was surprised because they actually started apologizing. But when another cab pulled up just then, they started screaming some mean things at the driver through his window, calling the guy a terrorist and trying to get on top of his cab.

A second later, the cops rolled up and I got back into my cab and watched as the dickheads were set straight.

I pulled out of there and cruised the empty streets for a while. The city seemed to be asleep already, but there were still some stragglers finishing up their long nights. I found my next passenger leaning on a parking meter on 14th Street. She was a very drunk middle-aged woman, and when I stopped for her, she could barely get into the cab, she was that wasted.

Over the course of the eight-minute ride, she asked me how old I was three times, if I was "real" four times, and if I was "Hispanic" five times. It was like our conversation was stuck on repeat, with her forgetting what we talked about every five seconds and asking the same questions over and over again. When I dropped her off on Second Avenue and St. Marks Place, and after she'd figured out how dollar bills worked while trying to pay me, she slammed the door and promptly fell onto the back of the cab, causing bystanders to gape and smirk. She finally found a mailbox to hang on to, and gave me a loopy little wave as I pulled away, thus satisfying my incoherent drunk quota for the night.

I was starving after finishing up my shift and dropping off the cab, so I stopped by a twenty-four-hour Indian restaurant near the garage that caters primarily to taxi and car-service drivers. On a shelf behind the counter sat a few huge jugs of White Horse scotch, which the waiter poured into paper coffee cups, diluting it with water or Canada Dry club soda, for on- and off-duty drivers alike. More than once already, I'd seen a car-service driver come in and do a shot with the waiter before taking his little paper-cup cocktail back to his black Lincoln and continuing on his shift.

This didn't much surprise me, since car-service drivers had a reputation among yellow cabbies for drinking on the job, as well as for being crappy, slow, unprofessional drivers in general. Car-service drivers usually drove black Lincoln Town Cars, though sometimes the cars could be silver or white, and they were a different kind of "for-hire vehicle" than yellow cabs in that they were supposed to respond only to dispatched radio calls. Customers would call the car service and ask for a car, and one of these would be sent. There was a lot of rivalry between us and them, though, because they were legally barred from picking up street hails—that was *our* domain— but they did it all the time anyway, giving rise to the term "gypsy cab." They cut into our business, which, in our collective opinion, was tantamount to stealing money directly from our pockets.

As I was sitting at the counter waiting for my to-go order, a man walked in with two empty Aquafina water bottles. He sat on the empty stool next to me and tried to start up a conversation.

"Did you have a good weekend?"

"It was okay," I replied.

"Do you live around here?"

"Sort of."

He pressed on. "Where do you live?"

I said, "Listen, I'm really tired and don't feel like talking, okay?"

He continued, "Well, if you need a ride, I'm a cab driver. I can take you."

I said, "No thanks. I have a car."

When the waiter came over, the man handed him the Aquafina bottles and gave his order in Hindi. The waiter proceeded to measure out two cupfuls of White Horse whiskey, pouring them into one of the bottles. The other bottle he filled with tap water. The man paid his bill and left, and I couldn't resist following him to the door to see which color his "cab" was, black or yellow.

Much to my dismay, it was yellow.

C H A P T E R   5

D riving a cab provides a rare view into people's lives. So many passengers are on the phone or carrying on a conversation with a companion in the backseat that they forget half the time that you're even there. Or, if they are remotely aware of you, they just don't care. Sometimes I suspect many passengers act this way because they assume their driver doesn't speak English. Cab drivers either erase themselves or are erased by the public. We become invisible people, to the point that our passengers feel free to talk about pretty much anything in our presence, right behind our heads, letting it all out as if they weren't in a filthy public car but in a cozy private room with no one else around.

On those occasional rides when we're not invisible to the passenger, as in when they're actually interested in us as people, we're still not full, complete human beings to them. Instead, we serve as partially blank screens for them to project their ideas onto, and, to get better tips, some of us even try to live up to their expectations.

What's good about this is that people are generally more open about themselves with a cab driver. They know the chances of ever seeing us again are pretty low, and there's a certain kind of intimacy that the space provides, making it an impromptu shrink's office in motion.

Unfortunately, in my cab, everyone who wanted to talk wanted to talk about *me*. I was an anomaly to them, so they wanted to figure me out, asking where I was from, what I did before, how I got into driving a cab, and why. They needed to understand it somehow, and they always assumed I was either a student or an actor. When they started in on these questions, I usually used it as an opening to turn the conversation around and ask about their lives. I'd say, "Okay, now you know all about me. So tell me what *you* do." Half the time they were bankers or lawyers. But the other half of my passengers held a wide range of occupations that I had never given much thought to before.

In New York City, you're defined not by who you are but by what you do. Sometimes people will tag a little disclaimer on after they tell you what their boring jobs are, like, "I manage hedge funds, but I'm really a writer."

Some of the people I've met in my cab included an undercover narcotics cop, an ironworker, a curator at the Museum of Modern Art, singers from the Metropolitan Opera, musicians from Lincoln Center, a receptionist by day/musical theater person by night, a federal judge, a massage therapist, a jewelry designer, bartenders, a private investigator, a doorman, a filmmaker, struggling actors, a few minor rock bands, a psychic, an animal oncology nurse (who administered chemo to rich people's pets), a makeup artist, and a man whose business card listed him as a composer, bassist, DJ, and multi-instrumentalist (I guess he was covering all the bases). The list goes on.

Incidentally, though many people were aspiring stars, I did have a few bona fide celebrities in my cab. Of course, it's an odd mishmash of a list and it includes such people as the wife of former New York City mayor David Dinkins; an up-and-coming singer/songwriter named Teddy Geiger; Justin Theroux, the actor from *Six Feet Under, Mulholland Dr.,* and *Charlie's Angels;* and, most notably, Jon Stewart of *The Daily Show.* In his case, I was so starstruck, I forgot to turn the meter on for nearly ten blocks, but he turned out to be a very modest, nice guy, and left me with a very decent tip.

Every cabbie has at least a few celebrity stories, and I was lucky in that all the ones I recognized were not jerks. But those star moments were few and far between. Most of the time the passengers getting into the cab were just regular people.

One night I picked up a woman outside Lincoln Center and took her downtown, to 11th Street and Fifth Avenue. On the way, she started asking me the usual questions, like, am I scared to drive at night? How old am I? Where am I from? And so on. After I blandly answered all her questions, she said, "You know, I used to be a cab driver, back in the eighties."

This got my attention. "Really? How was it back then? Those were much more dangerous times than now."

She said, "Yeah, but I guess I was lucky. I was almost mugged only once, but I managed to get out of the situation relatively unscathed."

"What happened?"

She unfolded the story. "These two guys wanted to go to Jamaica, Queens. Something just felt wrong, so halfway there, I demanded the money up front. They didn't want to give it to me. They started yelling at me to give them *my* money. I started speeding and honking, and managed to close the partition, until finally I hit a red light and stopped. They jumped out and ran away."

I said, "Yeah, nothing like that has happened to me yet, knock on wood, but I guess it still happens. Just not as much as it did back then."

She asked my name, and when I told her, she introduced herself. "My name's Michelle."

At the end of the trip, I was writing on my trip sheet, and she said, "Oh, you're a lefty too? So am I!"

At that point, I couldn't stop myself from getting weird. I said, "So, wait, your name is Michelle, and mine is Melissa," reaching for some sort of connection. "That's pretty close. We're both left-handed, and you used to be a cab driver. . . . It's like you're my future self!"

She said, "Yeah, but like twenty-five years older."

I said, "Okay, so, you have to tell me what you do now. What does my future hold?"

She answered, "I'm a doctor. I went back to school after driving the cab and became an M.D. I have a family practice downtown."

She gave me a nice tip, wished me luck, and got out.

Another time, I picked up a middle-aged woman on the Upper West Side. She was asking me the usual questions, and when I asked about her, she told me she was a psychiatrist.

"Do you like it?" I asked.

"I hate it."

She continued, "Actually, I used to drive a cab. I did it for four years back in the seventies to put myself through school." I thought she was joking and made her swear she was telling the truth. She didn't look like someone who would ever have gotten behind the wheel of a yellow cab, and I was convinced she was playing some sick shrink mind game with me, but she ultimately seemed sincere, and sincerely miserable.

When I asked her why she didn't just quit if she didn't like what she was doing, I realized just how dumb that question was. Why doesn't *anybody* quit their shitty jobs? The answer is simple: Money.

Her version of this was "I've got a family to support." She got out at a very fancy doorman building on the Upper East Side, wished me luck, and tipped a dollar.

Another former cabbie that I had as a passenger was a very old well-to-do white man. He told me stories about how cabs used to be considered part of the police department because the cops didn't have that many cars back then. Those were the days when cops would jump into a cab and actually say, "Follow that man," and off they would go, united in pursuit of some criminal trying to flee.

"Things are so different now," he said, and I agreed. I wondered aloud if things would be better for cabbies if the cops still felt we were on their side. We agreed they probably would be.

When I asked him what he did now, he told me he was a doctor.

I couldn't figure out what the connection was between cabbie and doctor, but it appeared that all signs pointed to some form of medical profession when one finished being a cabbie and moved on to the next thing.

There was another guy in my cab once who did do something I found myself very interested in. He said he had just gotten back from Iraq and was explaining how Americans had no clue what was really going on over there. When I asked him why he was there, he said, "Just as an adventure." I asked for more, and he told me he was the author of a few books on the world's most dangerous places. In fact, that was the title of one of his books, and it sort of served as a travel guide for people who wanted to visit parts of the globe that were in turmoil.

He had a Geraldo Rivera–like mustache, and I imagined that this was the guy Geraldo wished he was. He was the real deal. He didn't seem very impressed with me or my version of adventure, and in the shadow of his experiences, neither was I.

When I got home that night, I looked him up online, and sure enough, there he was, Geraldo mustache and all, with three books to his name and a long history of close calls on his life. He'd been in just about every modern war zone thinkable, and I felt an immediate attraction to what he was doing. Part of why I ultimately started driving a cab was because it required me to overcome my fear of doing something completely unknown, possibly dangerous, and inherently mysterious.

When I finally did become a cabbie, the job eventually became less romantic while the danger seemed to grow in some ways. It was certainly no Iraq, but I was slowly starting to see how this job could drive a person crazy.

I showed up at the garage one early afternoon to find Harvey sitting outside in the sun in a plastic lawn chair wearing a pink skirt and a white cardigan. I had already decided I didn't really like him. He always seemed to be sort of laughing at me, sitting there with his hands folded over his belly and smiling smugly whenever I talked. He just didn't seem to take me very seriously, and it certainly didn't endear him to me. I forgave some of this because he *was* exceptionally smart, smarter than me, to be sure, but he also came off as arrogant, like there was no use even trying.

There was even an instance when he refused to finish the story he was telling because I didn't know where the place was that he was talking about. He was going on about taking someone to the big Toys "R" Us in Times Square, the one with the Ferris wheel inside, and, still being so new, I said, "Oh, where exactly is that again?" Of course, looking back on this, I feel beyond dumb for not having known, but Harvey certainly didn't make it any easier for me.

He raised an eyebrow and said, "You don't know where the biggest Toys 'R' Us in the world is?"

I guess to him, with all his New York knowledge, it was like not knowing where America was. I backpedaled a little, sputtering to try to cover up my own ignorance, but it was too late. Harvey just shook his head like he'd forgotten who he was dealing with for a second. Then, without looking at me, he said, "Forget it," and walked away, like I was a lost cause not worth the effort.

In our conversations he also occasionally and inexplicably brought up the topic of sex, but without it being directed to me in any way. One time, when I complained of being out of it and tired, he said, "I only get tired when I don't sleep or when I have bad sex." I felt like he was testing me, trying to shock me or make me uncomfortable in some way, but it never worked. All it did was annoy me and make me develop even more distaste for him. But, despite all this, I still somehow gravitated toward him at the garage, mainly I think because he was always with Daniel and a few other guys I had gotten to know over the previous couple of months.

I pulled a chair next to him and sat down. He began, "How'd you do last night?"

I said, "It was fair. Business was steady for me until about midnight. After that it got slow, but I kept getting lucky. How'd you make out?"

"I didn't make out with anyone. But thanks for asking." And when I didn't respond to his joke, he went on, "I came back early after I hit those stupid dividers on Second Avenue by the Midtown Tunnel. So, I guess I didn't make out too well."

Apparently Harvey had a lot of accidents. I think he held the record for our garage, which was a pretty big accomplishment. Usually, if you have too many accidents, a garage will "fire" you, as much as any job you've never been hired at can fire you. Cab drivers are not considered employees; we're "independent contractors" and we pay the garage to let us use their cars. As long as the garage is making money off of you, and not spending too much on repairing any damage you may have caused, they'll keep you around.

For some reason, the owners, David and Lenny, liked Harvey, despite his many mishaps. He worked seven days a week, every single week, so in a way, that excused some of his collisions—given the law of averages and everything—but not all. And, because most of the accidents were minor and usually involved only inanimate objects, the garage was able to overlook them, since he wasn't *too* big an insurance liability.

He was starting to tell me about the dividers and why they shouldn't be there in the first place when "Fucking Harvey" came over the loudspeaker. Paul the crazy Romanian dispatcher seemed to have a particular antipathy toward Harvey, but I never knew exactly why. I assumed it had something to do with Harvey's choice of attire, but I also realized eventually that they had had enough screaming matches with each other that it couldn't just be the clothes. Paul abused everyone at the garage, but Harvey always fought back, and this only made Paul abuse him even more. There was certainly no love between them.

Harvey didn't seem fazed by it at all. He stood up and said, "See you on the streets, my dear," and left.

I got my cab an hour later and found myself on Orchard Street, a single-lane one-way just south of Houston, stuck behind a double-parked police van. The cops were standing on the sidewalk talking, and clearly had no intention of moving their van. I decided I could get by if I folded my side mirror in, but when

I reached out to grab it, the whole mirror just fell off in my hand and was left dangling by a couple of wires. This was not good. I tried replacing it, but I couldn't get it to stay on.

With the mirror in my hand, I managed to slowly and cautiously pull past the police van. I had just barely squeezed by and was about to pull over to try to sort out my little situation, when all of a sudden a cop ran up from out of nowhere and punched the hood of my cab. He was very young, probably younger than me even, and I judged by his lack of pins and stripes that he was most likely a rookie.

"Watch where the hell you're going! This isn't a fucking race!" he screamed. I was freaked out and completely confused. I had barely been moving. I just looked at him as he came up to my window and got in my face. He yelled, "You need to fucking RELAX." I had no idea where he'd come from or what he was talking about and I thought he must be kidding or something.

I could see his face was red and flushed as he again screamed, "FUCKING RELAX!" He was so close, some of his spit landed on my cheek, and I realized this was no joke at all. This guy was a lunatic. I felt a hot flush of my own anger and my entire awareness got caught up in a serious internal struggle. I was straining to defend myself, to yell right back at him, like I would with a normal person, but he was a cop. I knew there'd be trouble if I did. In what felt like a gargantuan effort, I reined in my anger and, instead, said very quietly, "I *am* relaxed."

He sneered at me and marched away.

I imagined that, being a rookie, this guy probably got abused and shit on around the clock by higher-ranking officers, not to mention the general public, and, in a trickle-down economy of anger, he was able to recycle some of that aggression by shitting on someone he could actually outrank. Since cabbies were at the bottom of the food chain, one of the lowest castes in the city, vilified and demonized by just about everyone, and holding no real power or respect, we were the perfect punching bags. And we had no one left to filter the aggression into.

To be sure, I'd never had so many problems with cops as I did when I became a cab driver. It was like I was driving a yellow target around the city, and police harassment was yet another thing I was just gonna have to get used to.

I found a parking space and pulled over. I tried reaffixing my mirror, but it just wouldn't stay. When I was able to get it perched precariously onto its hinge, I switched on my off-duty light and headed back to the garage.

When I got there, Jackson, the big Jamaican head mechanic, came out, and when he saw my problem, he just laughed. Taxi mirrors, like taxi drivers, take so much abuse on a daily basis, they're practically designed to absorb it. They are hardly ever truly broken, just knocked around, and they usually bounce back pretty easily. But I didn't know that yet, and I watched in awe as Jackson picked up the mirror, twisted it around, and snapped it back into place in a matter of seconds. Indeed, it wasn't broken. I just hadn't known how to fix it. The whole thing had been a total waste of time. But at least now I knew for next time, which there almost surely would be.

I raced back to the city and found a fare on Madison Avenue. She needed to go to 96th and First Avenue, so I headed uptown. At this point, it was 5:30, deep rush hour, and Madison was a crowded, roiling sea of traffic. I was anxious to make up for the time I'd lost going to the garage, so, ignoring the sign telling me turns were prohibited until 7:00 P.M., I crossed Madison's forbidden "bus-only" lanes and made a right turn onto 54th Street.

Cops often sit at these intersections, waiting for idiots like me to get desperate enough to make such a turn. And, sure enough, the cops were there that evening, waiting in an unmarked car. They got out as I passed over the crosswalk, and motioned for me to pull over. It was already a bad-luck night, and it seemed to be getting worse by the minute.

When one of the cops approached, he threatened me with three tickets—one for making the turn, one for crossing the bus lanes while doing it, and one for "failing to yield to pedestrians in the crosswalk." It was total bullshit. Then he looked at my license and said, "I can tell by your hack number that you're pretty new, but you should know the rules by now." He walked back over to his car to run my information through the system.

I sat in the cab and seethed. I was having a bad day. But it was my first bad day so far and I knew I needed to get used to it. This was just the tip of the iceberg, according to some of the stories I'd heard around the garage. I already knew that cops didn't ever give cabbies just one ticket. They piled them on, giving three, sometimes four, summonses, which put us in jeopardy of accruing too many points and potentially losing our licenses. We were easy targets for cops who needed to fill their ticket quotas, more so than regular cars, and this was another part of the package I wasn't so ready for.

When the cop came back, he said, "I'm gonna give you a break and give you two out of three."

Some break. He handed me the flimsy yellow pieces of paper and said, "It's a hard job. You haven't been doing it for that long, and hopefully you won't be doing it for much longer."

I took the tickets and kept my mouth shut. I couldn't afford any more trouble.

I was so frustrated, it took me a little while to calm down. As we drove away, I could tell my passenger felt bad for me. She was trying to talk and cheer me up. When I finally relaxed a little, I was able to hold a conversation with her. After telling her about my earlier run-in with the cops, I turned to her and said, "Yeah, my day is going so badly, I'll probably get into an accident next." She was like, "Oh, don't say that." I laughed and told her I was kidding, and we kept driving. I got her home without further incident.

An hour later, I was empty and heading down Broadway in the middle lane, going slow on my approach to a red light right near Columbus Circle, when I hit the car in the next lane over. It was a Nissan and it hadn't gotten fully over into the right lane. I thought there was enough room for me to get by it, but apparently there wasn't. As I pulled up to the light, the rear sides of our cars touched.

I didn't even feel the hit, it was that uneventful, but I heard it. There was a little crinkly-sounding crunch, and when I looked over, I saw an angry face in the driver's seat of the Nissan. I got out to make sure it had actually happened, and there they were, the rear sides of our cars just sort of kissing, swapping paint in the middle of Broadway. We pulled into the side street and started trading information.

The Nissan's taillight had a crack in it and some of the finish was scratched. The cab, amazingly enough, had no sign of damage whatsoever. No one was hurt and it was really no big deal, but still, it was my first accident, and the cumulative effect of the day was enough to completely shake me up.

I called the garage and got Warren, the cashier working that evening. I was relieved to hear his voice. Warren and I had become friends, and he always took good care of me. He was a sweet, smart middle-aged guy, a former cabbie as well as a former bartender, and he understood people like only someone who'd done both of those jobs can.

When Warren heard my frazzled voice, he said, "Just finish up there, hit your off-duty light, and come straight back to the garage. You're going home."

I was so nervous the whole way back to Queens, I drove probably about two miles per hour. I was totally spooked and thought I felt bad luck all around me. There was no way I could've continued driving for the night, even if Warren would've let me.

When I got back, Warren split the meter with me instead of charging me the $132 for the whole shift. This meant that, after gassing up, I got to keep a little less than half of what the cab's meter had earned for the night. I certainly hadn't broken even in the few hours I'd worked, so if Warren hadn't done me this favor, I would've ended up paying about $80 out of my own pocket to cover the lease fee. There's definitely nothing worse than going to work and actually *losing* money instead of earning it. As it was, I lost money on the night anyway because of the stupid tickets.

Warren knew it was my first accident, so he was extra nice, calming me down and comforting me a little bit. I asked him, "How often does this happen, accidents and stuff?"

He said, "About once a day."

I don't know why I was surprised. He continued, "Are you kidding me? We've got a hundred and fifty cabs, what are you gonna do? It happens all the time. Don't even worry about it. You're just lucky you didn't damage the cab. Then Lenny would really kill you!"

I filled out an accident report, paid out half the amount that was on the meter, and went home at 8:00 P.M. with $30 in my pocket.

CHAPTER 6

Night-shift cab drivers, along with sanitation workers, EMTs, and cops, have a special relationship with the city. There's usually a point in every shift when it seems like we are truly the only ones out there, the only people left awake—or at least it seemed that way to me. There was always an hour or two when business dropped off, screeching to a dead halt, and yet I kept working, cruising the avenues, waiting for the bars to evict their last drinkers, or the most stressed of the stressed-out office workers to finally give up and go home. Indeed, I never realized just how many people worked so late until I started taking them home at two or three in the morning. Of all those lights that are on all night in all those office towers, the ones that give us the famous twinkling New York skyline, I'd say a quarter of them are on because there are that many poor schmucks still at work at their desks.

These men and women were all tucked away in their offices while I cruised the quiet streets, looking to pick up the last random stragglers, watching the rats find their courage, watching the garbage get swept away by stone-faced sanitation workers, watching the police and the fire department and the EMTs take care of business, which always seemed to get busier for them in those small hours. After a while, it all builds up to create an intimacy with the city, a sense of ownership and familiarity that most daytime New Yorkers completely miss out on.

For me, it was a complicated relationship. Sometimes it filled me with wonder and joy, other times with anger, despair, and heartbreak. It was a love/hate connection that was constantly shifting but was always powerful, and it sometimes gave me the feeling that I truly knew this city, when, in fact, it's a city that can never truly be known by any one person.

When I was driving late at night, the streets belonged solely to me and the other cabbies. Every red light, every marquee, every upturned garbage can, spoke only to me and my taxi brothers. Everyone else was just a visitor, a tourist—there for a moment, gone the next. But we stayed, cruising until the city closed down for the night, sometimes even continuing on until it opened its eyes again at daybreak to start all over again.

My late-night taxi passengers consisted mostly of people going out to have their version of "fun." Like the yuppies—in their expensive sports jackets and casually contrived T-shirts, and their female counterparts in sexy low-slung dresses and tiny purses, stinking of perfume—who, without fail, got dropped off at the velvet ropes outside of some "hot" Chelsea club. Or the fancified middle-aged couples picked up outside one of the Waldorf's restaurants, smelling like freshly eaten steak, on their way to the opera house or the theater. Or the younger, less affluent hipsters, going to their concerts at Irving Plaza or Bowery Ballroom, with their iPods tucked away in their pockets, their collars turned up, and their sneakers laced just so. Or the less fashionable fraternity types, coming into Manhattan from the suburbs, who almost always went to bars on the Upper East Side or in midtown, or, if they were feeling particularly adventurous, on the Lower East Side.

And after that, it was all just different versions of the same people coming home from their nights out, all in various states of intoxication.

It often occurred to me that everyone was under so much pressure to have this vague thing called "fun" that going out was almost like a job itself. It seemed like such a grand effort, with everyone dressing up in special clothes, perhaps smoking pot, downing a few drinks, possibly indulging in a few bumps of coke, all in pursuit of this mythical "good time."

Sometimes, witnessing this parade of excited, dressed-up partygoers, it got to be too much and I could hardly bear it. The sheer repetition of it would be enough to spin me into an abstracted panic that it was all just passing time until we die, yet another arbitrary, meaningless way to get through the day. And, too often, when the post-party crowd got into my cab, all rumpled now and unbuttoned, I would feel sad and nervous and worried about the state of things, and then, of course, about the state of my own mind. Why couldn't I just enjoy enjoyment? It was even harder when half these people acted like unaware assholes, the drinks and the drugs having given them the sense that they were indeed the center of the universe, just like they'd always suspected. And my worldview was only reinforced, and I drove fast so I could get them out of the cab before they puked or passed out.

Of course, I'm no different. I usually need one or two drinks before I can partake in the fun-having myself. Which is all I really wanted to do the night after the whole tickets/accident fiasco. I wasn't quite ready to get back behind the wheel yet, but I was ready to get drunk off my ass and have my own "good time" for a change.

When my best friend, Allie, and I showed up at the Hole—a dirty, graffiti-covered dyke bar that conveniently ignored the newly enforced citywide smoking ban—I felt like a war hero. At that time, the Hole was the center of our little scene's nightlife, and it provided us with a seemingly endless supply of dyke drama, which is what kept it interesting, I suppose. There was bound to be at least one ex-girlfriend in attendance, or your ex's ex, or maybe even your most recent love interest, who just broke up with someone you're sort of friends with and who you probably shouldn't betray, or some other absurd combination like that. And we crammed ourselves in there practically every single weekend, never getting enough of it.

But that night, I felt like I'd just gotten my ass kicked a tiny bit in the harsh all-too-real outside world, and I had made it out in one piece—slightly traumatized and scared, perhaps, but intact all the same. I was feeling pretty proud of myself and I was happy to be among people I knew in a safe, familiar place. I was a little more energized and alive than usual, and all the regular drama and social bullshit of the Hole suddenly didn't seem as important as it usually did. I felt sort of aloof and above it all, and I was able to let this feeling feed into my newly inflated ego.

We arrived at midnight, and already all the old familiar faces were there. Through the smoke, a girl named Lisa emerged to greet me. She was an "artist," like most of the dykes there, and was friends with an ex-girlfriend of mine who I was not on particularly good terms with. Lisa spent her time making hip, overly obscure art that was understandable only perhaps to people with a master's degree, and that everyone else had to pretend to get, and that therefore was worshipped because it made them feel stupid. Lisa had always sort of ignored me until I became a "cab driver," which I guess counted as interesting to her. We were all just playing the roles of who we wanted to be, after all.

"Melissa, what's up!" She gave me a big hug and continued excitedly, "You still driving the cab? How's it going? Tell me some crazy stories!"

I wanted to snub her like she had snubbed me in the past, but I was feeling pretty impressed with myself and I couldn't resist the opportunity to show off. I pretended to be casual. "Oh, yeah, it's okay. You know. I got two tickets and had an accident last night, but . . . you know. No big deal."

The effect was as intended. Her eyes widened and she smiled and grabbed my arm. "Oh man. Are you okay?" I nodded and shrugged, like, *Yeah, whatcha gonna do.* She asked, "What happened?" and all of a sudden, I found myself exaggerating, slipping deeper into my role and trying to amp up the story, to make it seem exciting even though it had really just been shitty and frustrating.

"Well, first this dickhead cop like totally punched the hood of my cab because he thought I was going too fast. Then I got two tickets for making an illegal turn. And after that I got sideswiped by some prick in a Nissan."

Allie came back from getting a drink at the bar and rolled her eyes when she heard what I was saying. She'd heard the story fifty times already. She gave me a narrow-eyed look, conveying that she knew I was exaggerating for Lisa's sake. Unlike me, Allie had zero interest in people like Lisa. She couldn't have cared less. But I guess I still had something to prove because I relished the attention.

I continued, "So, yeah, the first ticket was for turning onto 54th Street before seven P.M., and the second one was for 'failing to yield to pedestrians in the crosswalk,' which is total bull-shit . . ."

I went on for another minute before I noticed Lisa getting bored. Her enthusiasm had visibly waned. She didn't really care about me and my traffic mishaps, and, really, who wants to hear about someone getting a stupid ticket?

When she realized I had stopped talking, she said, "Oh man. That sucks. . . . So, like, have you had any crazy passengers?" That's all anyone really wanted to hear about, after all.

"Huh? Oh, yeah. Totally." I tried to think. I conjured a memory from a month or two ago that I thought she might find interesting and continued, "So this stripper gets in my cab and . . ."

Lisa bought me a drink.

The rest of the night played out much the same way. I held court, having long conversations with random girls about my job and holding everyone's rapt attention. I basked in it, savoring the limelight, and the girls kept buying me drinks. At 4:00 A.M. the lights came on and I was wasted and feeling quite full of myself.

When Allie and I emerged from the bar, there was a line of taxis waiting on the curb to drive the last of the lesbians home. We got in one, opting not to trouble with the train that late at night, and told the driver we needed to make two stops in Brooklyn. The irony of now being one of these drunk late-night passengers in a taxi wasn't lost on me. I had had my night of "fun" and now it was over and time to go home. The spell of the Hole was broken by the cold outside.

Being in the backseat felt a little weird, and I was overly conscious of the driver, so I tried to be on my best behavior. I didn't want to be one of those annoying drunks. I remembered taking cabs a few months back when I first got my hack license, and how I used to want so badly to be part of it that I would somehow make it known to the driver that I, too, was a cabbie. I would use some sort of newly learned lingo that only a cab driver would know and then hold conversations with them about their night. I liked to think of myself as someone who *understood.* My friends would get annoyed with me for having to make a big production of the tip, since they saw it as me trying to make them feel bad and stupid, like *I* was the only one who could possibly know what a good tip was.

But I had been driving for a few months now, and the novelty of showing off to each cab driver I met had worn off. I was tired and didn't want to deal. I just wanted to go home in peace and not talk to the driver. I had already done enough showing off for the night.

Meanwhile, Allie was completely unaware of our driver, as most regular taxi passengers are, and was rambling on about the events of the night.

"Did you see that girl Kimberly? I totally wanna fuck her."

I was embarrassed. To her, the driver was invisible, might as well have been a machine, but I knew he was listening. That's what happens when you drive a cab. You get bored of the radio, bored of the horns honking, and you listen to your passengers' conversations, since that's where the real entertainment is. Most passengers don't realize or care if their drivers listen in, but I did.

I gave Allie a pleading look. I was trying to get her to stop talking, but she didn't catch on and continued describing the anatomy of this girl she liked. I realized that I had just gone from the role of "cabbie with stories" to "story" in a matter of minutes. I imagined the driver telling his friends, "So these two lesbians got in my cab and started talking about girls the whole way to Brooklyn. . . ." The thought made me cringe. I stayed silent and tried to tune Allie out.

I looked out the window and watched the city recede as we crossed the Williamsburg Bridge.

■　　■　　■

When I showed up at the garage the next day, I was hungover. I already knew it wasn't good to drive in that state, but I didn't have much of a choice. Driving with a hangover is almost as bad as driving while under the influence. I'd miss streets, take the wrong routes, miscount money. My head would be foggy usually until midnight, eight hours into my shift, which was when the hangover would finally fade. But in the interim, it sucked big-time.

I dragged my ass into the garage and saw Ricky first thing, smelling like pee as usual. When I walked past him, he said, "Hello, Melissa. I'm glad you're here. I want to show you something." He started fishing around in his shirt pocket for a while, and then said, "Oh, wait, I know where it is." He picked up his bag and pulled out an item shaped like a Windex bottle, but it was black and the label read URINE GONE! I wondered for a second why he was looking in his shirt pocket for this, but then remembered who I was dealing with. This guy had been driving a cab for way too long.

He was holding the bottle up proudly, offering it to me for inspection, but I just said, "Thanks, Ricky, but I don't think I really need that."

He replied, "You never know what someone's gonna do in your cab. It's good stuff. You can't get it in the stores. I had to get it from the TV."

I just smiled and nodded while the rest of the guys in the waiting room unsuccessfully tried to stifle their laughter.

Ricky went on, "I have a good urologist, if you need one."

I wondered if he thought I had the same problem as him. Or if he just didn't even realize that it was *he* who made the cab smell like urine every day, and not the passengers. In my experience, no passenger ever peed while riding in my cab.

One of the day cashiers who witnessed this exchange later

told me that he had once seen Ricky piss himself at the garage without giving it a second thought. He was sitting on a chair by the pay phone, and all of a sudden a stream of urine emerged from the bottom of his pant leg and trickled across the concrete toward the floor drain. Apparently it didn't faze him one bit—who knows if he even noticed—and when his cab came in later, he simply got in and went to work just like that.

I felt a little bad for him. Too many years driving had really taken a toll on Ricky. The guy could hardly walk on his own. He was a war veteran and had worked in the garment industry for thirty years before retiring. He drove a cab part-time during those years, and picked up more shifts after his retirement. There were rumors that he actually had money in the bank, a lot of money, and that he had a nice pension from his days at the garment factory, but if this was true, why was he still driving a cab? It was a mystery, and when I asked him about it, he was always vague. He was an old man, unmarried and probably lonely. If he did indeed have money, it was possible he continued to drive simply out of habit, or maybe just for the fleeting sense of companionship he got from waiting at the garage before each shift.

I was pretty sure Ricky's bladder and kidney problems were related to years spent holding it in behind the wheel. The nature of the job makes it so that you want to stop as little as possible because eventually business, or your luck, will run out, and you need to make your money while the going is good. Tons of cabbies have kidney problems from doing this, and many of the guys resort to peeing in bottles so they don't have to stop and get out of the cab. And since cab drivers don't get any form of health insurance—as "independent contractors," we would have to pay for it ourselves on a not-so-stable income—people like Ricky often don't have the money to spend on getting their kidneys fixed.

Later that night during my shift, while my hangover was

still in full effect, I waited at least four hours, until it was an absolute screaming emergency, before I finally stopped and found a bathroom. And it turned out to be a big hassle too.

I had a fare to LaGuardia Airport and expected I'd be able to use the bathroom there, but the taxi lots were all stripped—meaning empty of cabs, which is a rare gift—and I was unable to resist getting a passenger right away. I pulled up to the terminal and got a couple going to the Upper East Side. When they got out, another passenger jumped in before I even had a chance to hit my off-duty light. It was a short trip, though, and I dropped him off near a Dunkin' Donuts.

I parked at a fire hydrant, put my flashers on, locked up, and ran over to the store, just barely holding it in. Of course, they didn't have a bathroom. I tried the deli next door, but the cashier said, "No bathroom."

I was doubled over, about to lose it, and I pleaded with him. "It's really an emergency. *Please.* I mean, where do *you* go to use the bathroom?" He looked at me coldly and said, "Employees only."

I got so upset, I walked out cursing him, saying, "I hope you get a urinary tract infection one day."

I drove a few more blocks until I spotted a bar. As I ran straight to the bathroom before anyone could stop me, I fantasized about getting revenge on the deli guy. I wanted to stand in front of him at the register and say, "Oh my God, I can't hold it anymore," pull down my pants, squat right there, and pee all over his shiny linoleum floor, leaving a nice little puddle under the racks of Triscuits and Doritos. I should've totally done that. I really should've.

The next day, I realized the negative effects of holding it in for so long. Every time I had to pee that whole day, it felt like the biggest emergency in the world. My kidneys had been overtaxed and were revolting. I was worried I had done some real damage, but the following day, everything went back to normal.

Another bathroom crisis took place a few months before that, and I should've learned my lesson then. I picked up these two Orthodox Jewish women on Park Avenue, and when they told me they wanted to go to Midwood, Brooklyn, I was a little concerned. I already had to pee and this wasn't going to be a short trip.

I set out down the FDR figuring I'd be able to hold it at least until I dropped them off. Of course, it was rush hour, and there was a lot of traffic. By the time we got into Brooklyn, I was starting to sweat.

Driving became difficult. I was afraid I would have an accident in my jeans, and to prevent this, I began fantasizing about dropping the ladies off, pulling up to the closest parked cars I could find, and squatting in between them. The situation was so desperate, I no longer cared about things like privacy and safety and toilet paper.

After directing me around the neighborhood for a while, the women finally told me to stop. But only one got out. As the remaining woman told me I had to make another stop, alarms went off in my body as I passed the outer threshold of self-control. I was having a true physical emergency and my body entered the highest state of alert.

I tried to pull myself together while the second woman directed me to her house. But I began panicking again when she said things like "Turn at the light." I was trying not to breathe, but was forced to unseal my lips and ask, "Turn to the left or the right?"

"Oh, left."

She kept doing that, telling me to just "turn," until we finally made it to her house. She paid me, tipped nicely, and said, "Do you want directions back?"

I said, "No, actually, could you please tell me where I can find the closest public bathroom?" She paused for a second and replied, "Do you want to come in?"

I was surprised, but I guess I had sort of wished for this. I said, "Could I, really?" She replied, "Yes, it's fine. I've been there. I know how it feels."

I parked the cab and followed her into the house. She pointed me toward the bathroom and, while I was passing the kitchen, I saw a man with a yarmulke sitting there reading the newspaper. I didn't stop to say hi.

When I entered the tiny brown-wallpapered bathroom, with its shag-carpet-covered toilet seat and an AARP newsletter that had fallen into the sink, it felt like the most glorious moment of my entire life. I nearly cried. And when I left, I couldn't thank the woman enough. This was certainly the most generous tip anyone could have given me at the time. The whole way back to the city, I was filled with gratitude, mainly for the fact that I hadn't peed in my pants, but also for the reminder that sometimes humanity can, indeed, be humane.

When I returned to the garage the night of the Urine Gone, Ricky was already back. As I approached him, he seemed disappointed and said, "That stuff doesn't work so good."

I realized I needed to take a good look at Ricky and take heed. What had happened to him could easily happen to me. It was already starting.

CHAPTER 7

About two months into my cab-driving career, it was already clear to me that some people liked to use cabs not only as a means to an end, but also as an end itself. For some it even served a crucial part of their business, as was the case with the two young guys I picked up on 28th and Third. They wanted to go all the way downtown to Greenwich and Rector.

On the ride down, they were very polite and, as had already become standard for me by then, pointed out that I was one of only a few female cab drivers they had seen. One of the guys said, "Yeah, but actually, I had a young white female cab driver just last week."

When I replied with surprise at the odds of that, he said, "Well, I take cabs a lot." I asked why, and he answered, "I run a delivery service."

We headed downtown, and halfway there, one of them said, "We're just meeting a friend down there for a second. Would you mind taking us back to where you picked us up when we're done?"

I told him that I couldn't really spend the time waiting and he assured me that it would only be a minute, he wouldn't even be getting out of the cab, so I agreed.

When we were close, he made a call and I heard him say, "We're around the corner. Come down now." We pulled up to the designated spot and he pointed to a young preppy guy, saying, "There he is. Stop here."

The guy came up to the cab, and the delivery service guy rolled down the window. He said, "You wanted two *tickets,* right? Two tickets?"

The prep was like, "Huh? What? Oh, yeah, two *tickets.* Right."

An exchange was made through the window, and the guys in the back said, "Okay, let's go."

It was only then that I realized what this guy was delivering. It had to be coke. I mean, "tickets"? Please. But I kept my mouth shut about it, deciding discretion was the best option, not wanting to start trouble. Besides, what did I care, as long as I got paid?

As we drove back to where I'd picked them up, they discussed money and drugs, saying things like, "Yeah, man, remember when a thousand dollars seemed like a lot of money?" Hearing this, I just sort of assumed I would get a decent tip out of them. I debated over whether or not I should let them know that I knew what they were up to, offering some sort of a wink and a smile to show my complicity and professional discretion, trying to get them to pay me for my services, but again, I figured, why start something? Who knew where it could lead?

When we arrived back at 28th and Third, they paid, tipped $1 on the $20 fare, and took off.

So much for that.

At the garage that night, I told Harvey and Daniel about the dealers. Harvey was appalled that I allowed it. He said, "I would've collected the fare and kicked their asses right out. I don't want drugs in my cab. I don't let that kind of stuff happen in *my* backseat." I just shrugged my shoulders and smiled, a little shamefaced, like, *Well, I did it and it's done.*

He looked at me out of the corner of his eye and said, "You know, I have a daughter about your age. . . ."

"You have a *daughter*?" I could hardly believe that this man, in his black palazzo pants, stuffed bra, and low-cut yellow blouse, had children.

"Yes. Actually, I have *two* daughters. But my youngest is a recovering heroin addict. Or at least she swears to me and my ex-wife that she's not doing it anymore."

I didn't know what to say. Harvey continued, "So I have a zero tolerance policy for drugs, *in or out* of the cab. It hurts the industry and it certainly doesn't help the drivers. You, young lady, shouldn't let people get away with such things."

We stood there in silence for a second. Then another driver spoke up. He apparently was on the opposite end of the opinion spectrum in this matter. He didn't have a personal stake in the issue and didn't care what happened in his cab as long as he got paid, no one made a mess, and he didn't get in any trouble over it.

He shared a story about how he once let a guy smoke crack in his cab for $160. The guy got in, having just made his purchase, and asked to just be driven around while he smoked his drugs in the safety of the backseat. The driver refused at first, but then the guy handed him a wad of cash, and it was enough to change his mind. He also described how he'd taken people to buy drugs, waited for them with the meter running while they made their purchases, and then took them back to where they came from.

It took a few more months for that to happen in the back of my cab. The passenger was a thirtysomething pampered-looking white guy I picked up on the Upper East Side. He got in saying "Washington Square Park," which is an unusual destination. More often people name an intersection or an actual address. It's rare that someone takes a cab to a park. I thought it was a tiny bit weird, but didn't bother thinking too hard about it.

On the way down, he asked me how my night was going and I said, "Slow."

No matter how my night was going, I always said "Slow." This was for two reasons: (1) I wanted to encourage a sympathy tip; and (2) If anyone was thinking of robbing me, I wanted them to think it wasn't worth the trouble.

Anyway, he replied, "In that case, could you do me a favor and bring me back uptown after we get to the park? I just need to make a quick stop, but it shouldn't be more than five minutes."

It was truly a slow evening, so I agreed. When we got there, he got out and walked into the park. Two guys approached him, there was a transaction, and he came back to the cab, saying, "Okay, let's get the hell out of here."

I hit the gas and said nothing. Sometimes it was just best not to know, that way I could always claim my innocence if something went wrong.

We chatted on the way back uptown and he told me a bit about his life. He was an ex-pro snowboarder, a self-described "rich kid from Colorado." He explained that he didn't really have to work for money, but he had a restaurant job to keep his parents off his back and to make him seem responsible. He was a cynical, jaded young man with no clear direction in his life, and something about him disturbed me.

Halfway through the ride back uptown, he relaxed a little and said, "How ridiculous is it that I have to take a cab from the Upper East Side just to buy a dime bag from some niggers?"

I paused for a second and said, "I'd appreciate it if you wouldn't talk like that in my cab. I don't want to hear that kind of shit."

I could practically hear the smirk on his face as he said, "Oh, that bothers you? It shouldn't. That's what they are, peddling skunk weed and shitty crack in the park like that."

I said, "I don't see how *you're* so innocent in this situation, seeing as you were the one *buying* the weed from them."

"Well, I wouldn't if I didn't have to."

I was getting sick of talking about it, mainly because of his crappy racist attitude, so I just said, "Yeah, it *is* pathetic. You live in Manhattan. You really should have a delivery service if you're going to buy drugs."

He agreed, and we rode the rest of the way in silence. The meter was near $20 at the end of the ride and, I guess to show his appreciation for a job well done, he gave me a $5 tip. By that point, the tip almost didn't seem worth it. I wasn't bothered so much about the drug buy. It was more that the $5 seemed measly after having to put up with a bigoted ski brat. In my mind, it wasn't part of the bargain. I learned an important lesson: that sometimes the potential for a "large" tip just isn't worth the aggravation.

Only a few weeks after the snowboarder guy had bought his weed, I picked up a young white "punk" couple outside of CBGB (I don't even want to get into what an utter cliché this is). They wanted to go to Bed-Stuy and, on the way there, they

were discussing the subject of drugs. While going down Flatbush Avenue, they seemed to reach some sort of a decision.

The boy took out his phone and made a call.

"Yo, what's up, it's Jimmy. I need a bomb, yo." (A bomb, for
those who don't know, is slang for a bundle of ten bags of
heroin.) "No, it's *Jimmy*. You gave me your number a while ago,
and I came around there the other day. I'm the kid with the
leather jacket and tight pants, remember? . . . Yeah, can you
come to Franklin and Saint Marks? It's in Bed-Stuy. . . . Oh, all
right, yo. I'll see what I can do. I'll call you back."

He hung up the phone and said, "The car is being used by
someone else right now. He can't come to Bed-Stuy."

Then to me: "Yo, can we go to Williamsburg instead? We
need to go to South Third and Hooper." I didn't live too far
from there and immediately recognized this as the part of the
neighborhood that caters to the illicit needs of hard-core
junkies as well as casual dabblers.

The kid got back on the phone and told his guy they were
on their way, and the whole way there, the two in the backseat
talked about how they were going to get "the cure," and other
dumb shit that I'm sure made them feel very cool and hip and
William Burroughs-ish.

I already knew I wanted nothing to do with the transaction
that was about to happen. And I certainly didn't want them to
get their drugs and get back into my cab, where they would
probably do said drugs. I mean, taking a yuppie from the Upper
East Side to Washington Square Park to buy weed is one thing,
but taking dumb young punks to Brooklyn to buy heroin is a totally different scene.

When we pulled up to the corner they wanted, I immediately turned off the meter. The girl asked the guy, "Should we
hold the cab?" But I turned around and said, "No, I already
turned the meter off."

I wasn't really supposed to do that, but I'd rather break a TLC rule than have some kids shooting up or sniffing powders in the back of my cab.

I think the boy got the hint, though, because he indicated that they would find another taxi. They paid me and got out and went off to find their dealer, who should have recognized them by their leather jackets and tight pants.

Drug buys weren't the only seedy things to happen in my cab, but in terms of sex, I was lucky. Most of my passengers were able to contain themselves, holding off on the sex until they got home. But some came close—ha-ha, pun intended.

This middle-aged couple got in at Bleecker and Hudson, wanting to go up to 80th and York. I had seen them making out on the corner before they hailed me, and two minutes into the ride, the woman's head disappeared below the partition.

In the rearview mirror, I saw the guy sitting there with his head hanging forward. Over the sound of my low-tuned FM radio, I could hear a certain rhythmic breathing sound punctu-ated every now and then by wet, smacky, slobbering sounds. This very intimate noise made me uncomfortable. It was just weird. I would never expect a middle-aged Upper East Side couple to behave this way, but I guess it was their version of being "adventurous" or something.

But my main preoccupation lay with what was going to happen when the act was completed. As in, was she going to swallow, or were they going to leave a mess for me?

When we finally got to their nice doorman building, the woman popped her head up and paid the fare, tipping less than 10 percent. Cheapskates. A freakin' hotel room would've cost them *way* more than what they paid me. (Note to cab rid-ers: If you're so horny that you absolutely must fool around in a cab, tip your driver well. Seriously. You should reward us for not kicking your pervy impatient asses out, as well as for our tact and professionalism.)

When they were finally gone, I got out and apprehensively checked the backseat. To my relief, they left no visible evidence of their fun.

A few weeks later, I had the misfortune of being near the Lincoln Tunnel, where traffic was so backed up and gridlocked that me and my passengers and all the other cars on the street sat through six light cycles before we could get across the blocked avenue. Part of the problem was this big yellow moving truck that was blocking the intersection while sitting on the line trying to get to the tunnel entrance. I guess the driver got hungry or something because he actually GOT OUT of his truck in the middle of the intersection, walked across the street, and bought a hot dog.

Everyone on the block went nuts with their horns. No one could move, but the asshole just sauntered ever so slowly back to his truck while chewing his food. When he finally moved up, there was just enough space for the eastbound cars to squeeze through single file, so we all ran the red light and got the hell out of there after twenty long minutes of waiting. I should have known better by then—both the Lincoln and Holland tunnels connecting Manhattan to New Jersey are, without fail, traffic catastrophes every single day of the week. But the guy buying a hot dog in the middle of it all took the fucking cake.

Later that night, around 2:00 A.M., while I was buying my own hot dogs, there was a scene in Gray's Papaya. Two men walked in and tried to cut in line. A worker asked them to move over so the people ahead of them could order, and one of the guys took great offense to this. He started yelling at the top of his lungs, "Don't tell me where to stand! *No one* tells me where to stand!" His friend was laughing while trying to calm him down, and turned to the workers and said, "Give this man a hot dog!" The scene repeated itself two more times until finally it was actually their turn to order.

The friend turned to the yelling guy and said, "What do you want on your dog?"

The yeller yelled, "Put *every* motherfucking thing on it." Then, after giving it some more thought, he added, "And put some fucking pussy on it too! I want me a pussy dog!"

He got his hot dog, sans pussy, and started walking out, but not before yelling one more time, "No one tells me where to stand!"

When I got back to the garage that night, there was some buzz about a driver who had just been arrested. He was being held at the precinct down the street, and one of the mechanics went over there to retrieve the cab.

A few of us were hanging out bullshitting when he got back, so I asked, "What'd he get arrested for?"

The mechanic replied, "I'm embarrassed to say."

Stewie, a middle-aged Orthodox Jewish cabbie who lived in the Hasidic part of Williamsburg with his mother, was there and said, "What, was he picking up a hooker?" his accent dropping the *r* off the end of the word.

Yes, apparently he was.

I guess he picked her up where the prostitutes all hang out under the 59th Street Bridge, near Queens Plaza, but, alas, she turned out to be an undercover cop. In the conversation that followed, I discovered that this is not uncommon behavior for some cab drivers at the end of their shifts. Though, before that night I really had no idea about it. I guess I learned something new that day.

To my surprise, Stewie was the one educating me. I didn't expect this, given his religious observations and all. He had become my newest buddy at the garage, and I guess he felt comfortable enough with me by then to treat me like one of the guys. He was chuckling to himself, saying, "Imagine if it was me who got caught? I'd have to call my mother to come get me!"

I found out that the going price for a hand job under the 59th Street Bridge was twenty dollars. But when I asked Stewie how much a blow job might cost, he said, "No, you don't do the mouth. No mouth. It's not clean. Stick with the hands."

Two nights later, I picked up two very pretty, dressed-up young girls in Jackson Heights, Queens. This was good luck. It was already 1:00 A.M. and business was pretty slow, and it's rare to get flagged down out in the deeper parts of Queens and Brooklyn.

When they got in, they instructed me, in heavily accented voices, to take them to Queens Plaza. I dropped them off on the north side of the plaza and sat in the cab for a minute, filling in my trip sheet and debating whether I should go back to the city or quit for the night.

I watched the girls reach the crosswalk and stop. The area was totally desolate. No one else was around and nothing was going on except for the occasional subway rumbling by on the overhead tracks. The girls just sort of stood on the corner and I kept half an eye on them as I counted my money and organized my stuff.

After a minute or two, a nice silver Mercedes sedan pulled up from out of nowhere and idled next to them. The girls bent down and a short discussion took place through the window. Apparently having reached some sort of agreement, both girls got into the car and rode away.

One of the main activities at the garage while we're waiting for the day drivers to bring the cabs in is to stand around shooting the shit, telling cab stories, and talking about the job in general. Sometimes the conversations mainly consist of shoptalk, stuff no one other than a cab driver would find interesting. But when anyone has a good story, he makes sure to share it with his gang at the garage.

Of all the drivers there, Daniel had the best stories. A veteran cabbie, he'd seen pretty much everything.

One afternoon, a bunch of us were standing around as usual, when Daniel walked in and said, "Have I got a story for you!" His entire lean six-foot-seven frame was already laughing.

He continued, "So last night, a couple gets in around Meatpacking. They're visiting from Florida and they want to go to a hotel in Little Korea, but on the way they need to make a stop to pick something up at a friend's apartment." The details are important, but he left one out and someone interjected, "What time was this?"

Daniel thought for a second and said, "Oh, around eleven o'clock or so. Anyway, they ask me to wait, and, you know me, I don't like to argue, so I agreed. They were gone for about ten minutes, and when they came back to the cab, they were all of a sudden in a very good mood. It seemed like they were on drugs or something, but I can't say for sure. They start asking me, 'Has anyone ever had sex in your cab?' I say, 'Yeah.'"

He went on. "When they heard that, they said, 'Can *we* have sex in your cab?' I didn't know what to say, so I just said, 'What I don't know, I don't know. Do what you want, if you want to, as long as you don't make a mess.' So they start making out and I see in the rearview mirror the woman's head dip beneath the partition and I knew she was giving him a blow job. After a few minutes, she pops up and says to me, 'Can I come up there and masturbate in the front seat with you?'"

Daniel said no. He continued the story. "Then the guy says, 'We'll give you twenty bucks.'" At this point, Daniel made the sound of screeching tires. "Eeerrh! I pulled over to the curb and said, 'Come on up!'" The woman jumped into the front seat, hiked up her skirt, and started jerking herself off.

"So she's doing this, and I don't know *what* the guy is doing in the back, and everything is right there next to me in full view and they keep saying, 'Are you hard yet? Are you hard?' " At this point in the telling, Daniel laughed a little nervously and said, "To be honest, I wasn't. I felt a little bad disappointing them, but I just said, 'No.' When we finally got to their hotel, they begged me to come upstairs and have a threesome with them. I said, 'I can't, guys, sorry. But you have fun!' Then she pulled her skirt back down, they paid me, and got out!"

I knew Daniel well enough at this point to know he didn't lie. He really just didn't need to. The truth was weird enough.

I was almost a little jealous, thinking, *Nothing like that ever happens to me*. I began to realize that people were probably a little more reserved in the cab with me because I was female. But I wondered, did I *really* want stuff like that to happen in my cab? I wasn't so sure.

Still, in comparison to the guys at the garage, who masterfully told stories about women showing them their breast implants, about gorgeous lesbians making out in the back, about waiting outside shooting galleries for wealthy young addicts, and so on, my life in the cab felt a little dull.

Paul the crazy Romanian dispatcher once launched into a whole spiel about working the job to his advantage whenever someone wanted to use his cab as a no-tell motel on wheels. He said, "If it's gay guys, no problem. I just pull over while they're doing it and say, 'Guys, you do whatever you want to do, but this isn't a room, and I gotta get paid. I don't care what you do. In fact, I'm gay too' "—he's not—" 'but you gotta make sure I get taken care of.' " He continued, "They always give me the money after that, sometimes forty, fifty dollars. If it's some little white couple making out in the back, I do the same. 'Gimme the money, I gotta get paid.' People pay if you tell them to. I made so much money like that when I was driving a cab, the meter never mattered to me. Fuck the meter. You gotta be smart, okay?"

He ended this speech with his unique brand of wisdom, words that, at the time, had the ring of a Zen koan or a really smart fortune cookie, and words that I still carry with me to this day. He said, "Remember, Melissa, don't let anyone fuck you for free."

CHAPTER 8

It was a quiet Sunday afternoon in November and I was standing around at the garage as usual, waiting for the day drivers to bring the cabs back. Bush had just been "re-elected" a few days before and, on top of the hopelessness and depression that came with that shitty news, I had been sick for the whole week. It was my first day back to work, so I arrived early to try to get a jump on the night. There weren't many drivers around yet so I hung out and talked to Martin, Paul's eighteen-year-old nephew, who worked on Sundays as the cashier in the dispatcher booth, next to his father.

Martin and I were talking and somehow Harvey came up in our conversation. Martin asked, "You mean the gay guy?"

I replied, "Oh, he's gay?"

I don't know why, but it never occurred to me that Harvey might be gay. I just thought he had his shtick and took it to a really high level of performance. Either that or he was an old-school cross-dresser. He just didn't seem gay to me, but that could have been because he was so different from the gay people I hung around with. I did, however, notice that he changed his lipstick color daily and his nail polish weekly, which seemed superfluous if it was only for tips.

Martin looked at me like I was retarded and said, "Yeah. I mean, he wears women's clothes all the time."

Paul had been in the bathroom, and when he came back and heard what we were talking about, he joined in. "That motherfucker better not come on to me. I'll tell him, 'Fuck off, you sick fuck. Get the fuck away from me.' "

Something about all this didn't sit right. Women's clothing notwithstanding, I didn't think Harvey was gay, and even if he was, I couldn't imagine him ever making a move on someone like Paul. I said, "Are you sure he's gay? I mean, he's never said anything like that, and it always seemed pretty clear to me that he likes women. He told me he even used to be married. And he has two grown daughters!"

Martin said, "Why do you think he wears women's clothing? He *has* to be gay. Why else would he do that?" I didn't feel like explaining the intricacies of queer identity at that point, especially since they didn't seem to realize that I was a big homo too. I didn't care if they knew or not, but I certainly didn't feel like coming out to Martin and Paul just then. Not that it mattered, because Martin had already moved on to gossiping about another driver.

"You know that guy with the crew cut and the Rangers

jacket? He used to move coke by the weight. He was a major dealer but already had two strikes against him. If he got busted a third time, he would've done major time, so he went legit and started driving a cab."

I knew which guy he was talking about, had talked to him a few times. He had a wife and kids living in California, and he split his time between there and here, working for six months and then going back to his family for the rest of the year. He didn't seem like the type to be on the verge of major jail time, but who knows. The story sounded so unbelievable to me that I wondered whether Paul and Martin were having a little joke at my expense, testing my gullibility. It cast further doubt on the stuff they said about Harvey.

It was raining and I still felt sick and like shit when I got my cab. I was in a bad mood for most of the night. I couldn't stop thinking about Harvey and Bush and how fucked up the world seemed at that moment. I felt bad for Harvey somehow. What those guys said about him at the garage seemed so hateful, it made me wonder what they thought about *me*.

I spent the night coughing and sniffling in the front seat, feeling crappy. I'd been getting sick a lot lately, I think mainly due to the stress and long hours in the cab, and from touching the dirty smelly money all night, which always turned my fingernails black by the end of each shift.

Being sick lowered my tolerance for any sort of aggravating or annoying behavior on the part of my passengers. And it didn't help matters any when a drunk married couple got in the cab. Clearly thinking himself to be a liberated and provocative little devil, the man kept asking me if I'd like an "ass-slapping."

I might've found this almost funny had I been in a better

mood, so I tried really hard to be a good sport about it because they were drunk and I didn't have the energy to get offended. I just kept expecting the woman to say, "Okay, that's enough now. Let's leave her alone," but she never did. Instead, at the end of the trip, as she was getting out after her partner, she paused for a second, turned to me, and said, "He really does give a good ass-slapping."

The night only got weirder from there. The city seemed especially quiet and depressed in the wake of Bush's big victory. The darkness looked even darker, the rain even more portentous, and the vibe was enough to make anyone want to go home and hide. I picked up some tourists from Texas and we started talking about the election. We discussed red states and blue states and finally, stupidly, I asked them, "So, who'd *you* vote for?"

They answered simply, "W."

I knew even before I heard their answer that I shouldn't have asked. It's not wise to get into political discussions with passengers, unless of course you agree on everything. But if you disagree, all it does is cause added aggravation or a horrible argument, which can sometimes end with a complaint against the driver being logged with the TLC, which in turn leads to a fine. And with the election so recent, sitting on New York's heart like a fresh wound, it could've turned out even worse.

I just said "Oh," kept my mouth shut, and tried to get them out of my cab as fast as possible.

My next passenger was a young affluent gay guy going to meet his boyfriend at the Four Seasons Hotel. On the way, he told me all these stories about his love life, and all the things that he and his boyfriend argued about. The boyfriend, it turned out, was the heir to a major power-tools fortune and was disgustingly rich.

I was relieved to have a blue-stater in the backseat again,

so I started telling him about the Texans I had just picked up. When I got to the part about how they'd voted for Bush, he cut in and said, "Well, I didn't vote, but if I had, I would've voted for Bush too."

I couldn't stop myself. "But you're *gay*," I said. "Why would you vote for someone who hates your guts?" He replied, "I just don't trust Kerry. And besides, Bush does a lot of good things for business. My boyfriend's mother knows him and he's actually a really good guy."

Right. Of course. I guess money trumps sexuality when you live in that tax bracket.

When I dropped him off at the Four Seasons, the meter read $8.10. He gave me a twenty and told me to keep the change.

I put my politics aside and took it. In *my* tax bracket, money trumped convictions.

CHAPTER 9

I was on the streets for the first big snowfall of the city that winter. Scared off by the slippery streets, most other cabbies bailed out and went home. I grew up driving in New York snowstorms, so I stayed out and just took it slow. Only a few other cabs were out there with me, so I always had a passenger and was able to earn a decent wage that night, even despite the five-mile-per-hour speed I had to maintain.

One of my first passengers of the night was a girl from California. We drove along in silence while she looked out the window. The snow was falling in massive chunks, sticking to the ground, laying a pristine white carpet over everything. At points it even appeared that my tires were the first ones to ruin this little layer of perfection, pushing the snow to the side, making dirty parallel tracks down the avenue.

After a while, the girl looked up and said, "You know, I've never seen snow before. This is my first time."

I had simply been trying to navigate through it, treating it like just another road hazard I had to deal with, but when the woman said this, her sense of wonder became contagious. I remembered waking up in the morning as a kid and seeing snow out my bedroom window. My sister and I would sit in the kitchen and listen to the list of school cancellations on the radio, and when they announced our district, we would run outside to enjoy the freedom. I couldn't imagine what it was like to grow up, as this woman had, without "snow days."

There was hardly anyone out on the streets at all and it inspired a feeling of peace and solitude that is beyond rare in this city. In a place as loud as New York, this kind of quiet was so profound it almost seemed reverent. Not wanting to break the spell the snow was casting over us, we, too, remained silent for the rest of the ride.

Later in the shift, I drove a twenty-three-year-old gay boy named Matthew to his home in Chelsea. We were together for a while, since I couldn't shoot around the streets like usual, and after a few minutes, we started talking. Somewhere in the conversation, Matthew revealed that he had lost his virginity just the night before to a "self-proclaimed spiritual guru."

He told me the guy was a creep, and I looked at him and said, "Why'd you sleep with him, then? You're totally cute, you could totally get guys."

He replied, "No, I can't. I'm fat and hairy."

I took another look at him and said, "I can't tell from here if you're hairy, but you're definitely not fat."

He explained by saying, "Yeah, I'm not fat now, but I used to weigh three hundred pounds. I lost most of it, but now I have a lot of extra flesh all over my body."

I felt his pain. All those Chelsea boys were obsessed with waxed chests and hard bodies. I said, "You need to go where the dykes go, in that case. All the fags who hang out at lesbian bars are way more relaxed and cool." I listed off the bars and clubs he should try, where he could maybe meet some nicer, less superficial boys, and then we moved back to the subject of his freshly lost virginity.

He told me the sex was awful and the guy was a total sleaze-ball, but he'd just wanted to get it over with. Then he elaborated, saying, "Well, actually, I only *half* lost my virginity. I fucked him, but he only 'said hi' but didn't fully fuck me, so I guess I'm still part virgin after all."

When we finally pulled up in front of his building, I felt like we were already old friends. A year later, I ran into him again at Metropolitan, a gay bar in Williamsburg. He approached me and said, "Excuse me, but are you a cab driver? I think you drove me home last winter in a snowstorm!"

I remembered him and said, "Yes, I did!" And then, "So, are you still having guy trouble?"

He answered, "Yeah, you know . . . But it's getting better. At least I'm not sleeping with shitty spiritual gurus anymore."

Later in the snowstorm, I got into a fight with some rich tourists wrapped in furs down by Ground Zero. They were freezing out there but the streets were icy and there were five of them. I told them I couldn't legally and safely put them all in my cab since the legal passenger limit was four. I'd broken this rule many times before, but that night it just would've been too dangerous and too hard to stop on the ice with that much weight in the cab.

So these people, who were "doing Ground Zero" as part of their vacation itinerary, actually yelled and cursed at me for refusing to take them back up to the Plaza Hotel. When I told them they should split up into two cabs, they said, "The cab down here took all of us. What's wrong with you?"

When I insisted that I still couldn't risk it, they got more and more upset and we exchanged barbed words through the window, until finally they took aim and said, "Well, *you're* just a cab driver!"

I couldn't believe they were actually too cheap to take two cabs, but I shouldn't have been surprised. I had already learned that rich people were the stingiest passengers out there.

Despite my armor, their comment stung a bit, so I started rolling the car away as I replied, "Well, at least I'm a *warm* cab driver."

I closed my window, cranked the heat even more just to drive the point home to myself, and skidded away.

When I got back to the garage and turned in the cab at the end of the night, all I wanted was my bed. Unfortunately, when I went to unlock the Buick, I discovered the doors were frozen shut. I lit matches under the lock, kicked at the handles, and generally cursed and abused the car, but I still couldn't get it open. I ended up getting one of the mechanics to help me and we just punched and slammed on the doors together until the ice cracked.

When I finally warmed up the car and left the garage, I was freezing and exhausted and looking forward to home. I was halfway there when the car spun out on a curve, revolving 180 degrees so that it ended up facing the wrong way on a one-way street in Williamsburg.

I didn't get stuck there, though, and I didn't blow a tire, and there was only a minor dent from where I hit the high curb, so I guess that was lucky too. But still, the irony was not lost on me that I had survived the entire night in the cab without incident, only to end up spinning out in the Buick on my way home.

■   ■   ■

A week or two later, I acted as an ambulance for two girls who needed to go to the emergency room at Beth Israel Hospital, and it gave me a nice little sense of importance. It actually wasn't a huge emergency or anything, but I was into the idea of pretending we were going there on Urgent Business.

The reality was that one of the girls, oddly, had a sea urchin stuck in her foot, which she had acquired a week before while vacationing in Puerto Rico. It was causing an infection that prevented her from walking without pain, so she and a friend decided it was time to catch a cab to the ER.

I got them there quickly and in one piece and moved on to my next fare, who had an emergency of her own, though of a different caliber. I overheard her on the phone explaining to a friend how she was rushing over to her boyfriend's house to have "makeup sex." It sounded important enough to me, so I got her there as quickly as I could. Urgent Business, indeed.

Later, I picked up a thirtysomething couple at the Hotel Gansevoort, a fancy hotel and bar down in the Meatpacking District that catered to upscale yuppie types who liked to think of themselves as fashionable. This couple needed to go somewhere in midtown and, on the way there, the girl looked at my hack license—which was displayed on the partition behind my head—and said, "I know a Melissa Plaut."

We were at a red light so I turned around to get a look at her face. I didn't recognize her or anything, so I said, "Really? That's pretty weird. It's not like it's a common name or anything."

She continued, "Yeah, but this one was from Rockland County."

Okay, that was just too much. She *had* to be talking about me, but I had no idea who she was.

I said, "Uhhh, yeah, that would be me. I grew up in Rockland. Who are you?"

Her name was Juliette Thayer and she was a year older than my older sister. I don't think we had ever actually met, but her younger brother had been in my grade. Who knows how she even remembered my name.

All of a sudden, I felt an incredible sense of embarrassment. It was like, I could see her seeing me and thinking, *Melissa Plaut ended up as a cab driver, how sad,* and not seeing the adventure that I saw in it. This type of occupation didn't exactly line up with Rockland County's middle-class ideas of success and happiness. I was born and bred on those ideas, but somehow I could never seem to make them fit in my life, no matter how hard I tried. Still, it wasn't easy to totally give them up and make the shift into something that worked for me—and this embarrassment was a remnant of that rejected paradigm, bubbling up from my childhood expectations, and what I imagined to be the world's expectations of a college-educated middle-class girl.

I have an old cassette tape that my dad made in 1982, when my sister was ten and I was seven. He had bought a microphone, had plugged it into his hi-fi stereo, and was testing it out by interviewing us. When he asked my sister what she wanted to do when she grew up, she said, "Be a doctor." She's now a pediatrician in California, married, and has a two-year-old son. When my dad asked me what I wanted to do when I grew up, I paused, thought for a second, and said, "Make love."

That pretty much sums it up.

I mean, I'm aware that I was totally projecting that night in the cab. Still, I couldn't help but imagine that this job was the lowest of the low in Juliette Thayer's eyes. It's like the proverbial story of the cool guy who graduates from high school only to remain living in his parents' basement and working at the local gas station. It's called a Waste of Potential, or a Lack of Ambition, or No Future.

I imagined Juliette saw it the same way my parents saw it,

except my parents knew me and, to some small degree, they understood my reasons. They knew I didn't *end up* as a cab driver—I *chose* to be a cab driver, and it wasn't like I was planning on doing it forever.

Of course, when talking about this with my father, he related a scene from a movie he had seen recently. The actor Jamie Foxx played a cab driver in Los Angeles that got taken hostage by Tom Cruise. My dad especially liked to point out the part when Jamie Foxx explained how he was only driving a cab temporarily until he could get his own business started up. Tom Cruise asked, "So, how long you been doing this?"

Jamie Foxx answered, "Eleven years."

My dad found this very funny.

I did not.

This was my adventure, a stop along the way to what I hoped would be further adventures. And, Juliette Thayer be damned, I wasn't going to let anyone take it away from me.

I couldn't wait to get her and her husband out of the cab. The whole ride I could just picture her telling her brother she'd seen me, and him telling all these people I went to high school with, and the idea of it just sort of made me feel gross. I wanted to explain myself, but there wasn't time, and where would I begin?

Fuck it, I thought. *Let them think what they want. They'd never get it anyway.*

CHAPTER 10

The holidays were quickly approaching. The lights at Macy's were already lit, and the city was busy erecting the tree at Rockefeller Center. The big twinkly snowflake had just been installed over the intersection of 57th and Fifth, though that wasn't lit just yet, which created a feeling of anticipation. It just hung there, suspended over all the cars rushing by underneath. Unlit, it looked a little sad, like it was waiting to burst to life, waiting for the moment it could tell all of New York that the holiday season had officially begun.

I'd never been a big holiday person, and I always thought it suspicious that people became more thoughtful and compassionate just because it was a certain time of year, but it was hard not to be seduced by it. With all the traffic and tourists and aggravation that came with that time of year also came an extra dose of kindness and appreciation on the part of taxi riders. I dove in, fully aware that, despite all the crowds and cars, November and December were the time to make enough money to get you through the slow months of January and February.

I picked up four visitors from Kansas City outside Elaine's. There was a homeless guy hanging around, trying to get money for opening people's cab doors for them. He was really working it, perfectly imitating a professional Upper East Side doorman, even bowing a little, and wishing everyone a good night and, of course, a very merry Christmas. He was quite convincing except for the small fact that he was dirty, dreadlocked, and dressed in rags. He opened the door for my passengers as I pulled up, and they tipped him eight whole dollars.

When they got in, I said, "I'm clearly in the wrong business. That guy's making more money than me!" They laughed and we were all in a good mood for the rest of the ride. When I got them to their hotel, they paid the fare and tipped me generously, though not as much as they gave the homeless guy. But it didn't matter. They were happy, and so was I. And so was that homeless guy.

Later that same night, I took a woman to the Upper West Side. The fare was $9.70. She handed me $13 and said, "That's the best driving I've seen in a cab—ever."

I thought, *This holiday spirit stuff isn't so bad after all.*

A week or so later, both the tree and the big snowflake had been lit and the New York holiday season was fully under way. An elderly couple got in my cab uptown. They were on their way back to Philadelphia and needed to catch their train at Penn Station.

Along the way, they revealed that they were the owners of

a semi-major potato chip company. We chatted about chips for a few blocks and how their business was affected by the whole low-carb craze. Then they asked if it was possible to drive down Fifth Avenue so they could see the tree on the way to the train station.

Traffic was an utter nightmare around there all through December, so I lied and said, "I wouldn't bother, if I were you. You can't even see the tree from the street anymore."

They accepted my advice and I drove them through Times Square instead. They were sweet and gave me a nice tip.

Later, while sitting in a traffic deadlock on Fifth Avenue by Rockefeller Center, I caught a spectacular view of the tree and listened to the blasting Christmas music, and felt a little twinge of guilt. Clearly I only appreciated this holiday spirit business as long as I was on the receiving end of it. I had been too selfish to dole any of it out myself.

Two days before Christmas, I picked up four black teenage boys in Times Square. They wanted to go to 86th and Third Avenue. They were rowdy and having fun and playfully cursing one another out the whole way up.

When we pulled up to their corner, they all piled out until only one of them was left standing there with the back door open. He called after his friends, "Yo, gimme some money, yo! I ain't paying this all by myself!"

When I heard that, I knew he was going to try to skip. I put the cab in park and called to him, "You owe me nine forty. And you better pay me right now."

He replied, "But they didn't give me any money. I'm not paying it all myself."

I said, "I don't give a shit, get it back from them later."

He answered, "You don't understand, it's impossible to get them to ever pay me back. They'll never do it."

I told him that wasn't my problem, but he'd already started walking away, saying, "I'm just gonna go get the money from them. I'll be right back."

I jumped out of the cab and started yelling after him, "Hey! Get back here and pay me! I'm gonna call the cops!"

Meanwhile, the streets were busy and people were trying to get into the cab. I could've just taken the next fare and made up for the loss pretty quickly, but I was enraged. Who the hell were these kids who thought they could get away without paying? I wasn't going to let them get away with it. It was only $9.40, but I was more concerned with the principle of it.

Some bystanders approached me and pointed to a fast-food place in the middle of the block. "They went in there." I jumped back into the cab and pulled around the corner in front of the restaurant.

Another cabbie, an older Pakistani guy, was standing there next to his cab talking on the phone. When I got out, he said, "Did they rip you off too? I had four girls in my cab and they went inside. I'm on the phone with the police."

I locked my doors and ran into the fast-food place yelling like a crazy person, "I'm gonna call the cops! I'm calling the cops right now! You better pay me!"

I was confronted with about fifty rowdy teenagers daring me to do it. They took one look at me and started saying, "Go ahead, whitebread, you wanna identify *me*?" and "Get the fuck out of here, you stupid white bitch," and other such compliments.

I looked around and was swarmed by boys and girls, but I couldn't seem to recognize which ones had been in my cab. I never really took a good look at them. I stood there yelling some more until finally I saw the boy who'd been left holding the door, the one who had been abandoned by his friends. I walked straight up to him and said, "I am going out and getting the cops and I'm going to identify you and only you. If you don't pay me, your friends won't get in any trouble, *just* you." He stood there raising his chin at me, daring me to do it, and defiantly protecting his tough-guy image for the sake of his peers.

As I walked out, the place was roaring behind me with riled-up teenagers. The Pakistani cabbie was still standing there, waiting on the phone with the cops, but I saw a cruiser at the light on 86th and I flagged it down. When I told the cops what had happened, they acted like they couldn't be more bored. They walked casually over to the restaurant with me, and when the teenagers saw them through the windows, the kids all started pouring out of the place.

The kid I'd identified came out with the crowd and said, for the cops' benefit, I'm sure, "I *told* you I was gonna pay you."

The cops just stood there and watched without saying a word. "How much was it again?" I should've added extra money on for the time I wasted going through all this crap, but stupidly I said, "Nine forty."

The kid counted out ten crumpled-up singles and handed them to me, and then said, "You best damn give me my sixty cents change!"

For a split second I remembered that morning when all the cabs in front of me passed those two black guys on First Avenue, and I wanted to say to this kid, "THIS is why cabs don't pick up black people." But right as the thought entered my head, I was immediately filled with disgust for myself for even thinking it. I was supposed to be different. Angry as I was at these kids, that was not who I was or how I really felt deep down. It was just anger, and the cheapest, easiest, most hurtful thoughts always seemed to come hand in hand with it.

I counted out the kid's sixty cents and got back into the cab to continue my night. So much for holiday spirit. I suppose I got what I deserved.

Chasing these kids may not have been the smartest thing in

the world to do, but I was so pissed off, I didn't care. In taxi school, Frank Roberts had given us a list of fourteen safety tips that included such vague wisdom as "Tip 2: Use a map when traveling to areas of the city you aren't familiar with." Or, "Tip 3: Beware at stop signs and red lights; thieves sometimes target these areas." (No comment on how stupid that one is, since, like, duh, stop signs and red lights are pretty much EVERY-WHERE.) Or, "Tip 9: Never admit to a customer that you're having a good shift." Or the one that I probably should've heeded this night, "Tip 13: Never follow a fare-beater into a building."

That night, I added a tip of my own: "Be wary when picking up teenagers. They think they are invincible and have no sense of consequences."

The safety list also offers new drivers the following: "Tip 14: After leaving the garage, be careful when walking to your car or taking public transportation." I realized soon after this incident just how important this piece of advice was. Luckily I didn't learn it firsthand, but secondhand was close enough.

I pulled the cab in late one Sunday night/Monday morning after my shift and heard the news that another driver had been mugged and stabbed just a little while earlier while walking from the garage to his car. Long Island City is sort of an industrial ghost town late at night. Usually, the only people around are the cabbies that are pulling in after their shifts and the occasional patron of the go-go bar that sits next door to the garage.

The story went that two guys approached the driver on an unlit street and asked him for directions. When he stopped to help them, they pulled out a knife, stabbed him in the kidney, and took all his cash. He survived, but they left him with an ugly wound in his back and he was laid up in the hospital for a few weeks. He returned to work after a couple of months.

It was clear that these guys were staking out the garage. The criminals knew that the night drivers walking to the subway or their cars after a shift were an easy target for some quick cash. I learned later that this happened sporadically at all the garages around town.

Not long after that, Harvey got mugged on the G train on his way home to Brooklyn. Luckily for him, it was a nonviolent mugging, and the guys just grabbed his money and ran into the next car, getting off the train at the next stop. It was five in the morning and I guess he just wanted to go home after that, because he didn't call the cops. What were they gonna do anyway? The kids would've been long gone by the time the cops showed up.

It was also around that time of year that a woman was raped on the platform of the G line late one night. It happened in Queens, somewhere near the garage, and it was all anyone talked about for a few days. Shortly after that, Stewie told us he'd seen the rapist on his way home one night.

A creepy-looking character approached him on the platform and started talking to him. He showed him pictures of naked girls on his cell phone and Stewie just stood there waiting for the train. The guy fit the description of the rapist to a tee, with a mustache and everything, but Stewie didn't call the cops. Instead, he just got on the train and went home.

Unfortunately, cabbies are all too aware of the powerlessness of the police. Often, when called, there's not much they can do—or *want* to do, as the case may be. When it comes to cabbies, a lot of cops seem to have a real antipathy. I'd always wondered exactly why this was, and then I got a clue when a friend of mine did a police ride-along for journalism school. I gave her instructions to uncover the roots of their cabbie hatred, and she came back to me with, "They said you guys drive like shit and that cabs never get out of their way when they're on an emergency call." She said she'd even witnessed this herself on the ride-along, but she also noticed that the ones not getting out of the way were all black Lincoln Town Cars from car services.

But the cops' biggest problem with yellow cabs was that there were just too many of them. True, there are about thirteen thousand yellow cabs on the streets at any given time, but that's not *our* fault. It's the city and the TLC's fault for putting that many out there. And this is what, in turn, forces us to drive with a little more aggression—or "like shit," as they seem to be so fond of saying—because every single one of those cabs is our competition for business, and when it comes to money, you do what is necessary to make sure you make it.

There were definitely some cabbies who pushed the limits of safety and decency and went over the edge—and of course they got all the attention and gave the rest of us a bad name— but the majority of the forty thousand hacks on the streets did their best to keep it safe while driving with the necessary efficiency and speed in order to make it worth it. Really, it's just a different *style* of driving, and I would even go so far as to say that cabbies, being more aware of their car and its limits, are better drivers than most "civilians."

Unfortunately the NYPD didn't quite see it this way. They also apparently didn't see the difference between car service cars and yellow cabs, so they ended up hating us all equally. So when something happened where the cops had to be called, like an accident for example, they usually blamed the cab driver, no matter who was truly at fault. They rarely ever gave us a break.

This made it always seem like such a hassle to call the cops, even when we weren't in the cab, like Stewie that night on the G platform. And, especially after a shift, we're tired and burned out, so if something bad happens, we usually just want to go to the safety and privacy of our homes and forget about the world.

As for me, after particularly frustrating shifts, I usually just went home and played Grand Theft Auto, getting intoxicatingly lost in a virtual world where I could run over people with impunity and beat the shit out of anyone I pleased, doling out justice my own way.

No thanks to Stewie, the G-line rapist was eventually caught.

A few months later, I read in the *Daily News* about a cabbie named Mamnum Haq who got stabbed by a passenger in his cab. It was all over the local news for a few days and the story went that he picked up a twentysomething white guy in Carroll Gardens, Brooklyn, and drove the guy to Brooklyn Heights, a well-to-do neighborhood that didn't usually see too much violent crime.

When they got to the guy's destination, the passenger reached through the partition and stabbed Haq in the shoulder with a six-inch knife. He wasn't even trying to rob him or anything—the guy was just crazy, it seemed. Then he got out and ran away and Haq fell out of the cab screaming for help. He was rushed to the hospital and he eventually recovered.

In a press conference, Matthew Daus, the commissioner of the TLC, practically put the blame on Haq, saying that if he had kept the window in the partition closed, the attack could've been avoided. In my mind, this was akin to blaming a rape victim for her rape by saying she shouldn't have been wearing a skirt.

It didn't make any practical sense to keep the partition window closed. Sure, it was bullet-resistant, and it separated the front from the back of the cab to protect drivers from potential attackers, but if you closed it, you couldn't hear what your passenger was saying. And besides, most people thought it was rude if you closed it on them and would get offended. In my time driving a cab, I only closed the partition once, and that was to drown out the stupid drunk guy who kept accusing me of being Italian after Italy won the World Cup, and who insisted on singing Pearl Jam songs at the top of his lungs in the backseat. Other than that, I always kept it open. Besides, if a cabbie picks up four people, one has to sit up front next to the driver, and what good is the partition then?

The day after Mr. Haq was attacked, everyone at the garage was saying stuff like "Just don't let anyone sit up front with you" and "Be careful who you pick up these days. There's a lot of shit going around right now."

The whole story made me nervous. And, of course, my first passenger that day banged on the front passenger-side window, indicating he wanted to sit up front with me. Of course he did. Today of all days.

He was a clean-cut older white guy with a cane. I rolled down the window and said, "You have to sit in the back."

He took great offense at this and said, "I'm a cripple," and held up his wooden cane to illustrate. "You have to let cripples sit in the front. It's the law." It was true. It was indeed the law.

I took a deep breath and wondered if I was being scammed as I unlocked the front door. I was on guard, but the ride passed without incident and I made it through the rest of the shift relatively unscathed.

CHAPTER 11

After New Year's the city calmed down a bit. Traffic eased up immensely, which made driving easier, but all the tourists were gone and business was dead slow. Most people had spent their savings on holiday shopping and were now scrimping and cutting down on expenses either by not going out as much or, when they did go out, by not taking cabs. It's like that every January. A slow month. Nothing to do but drive.

Cabs lurked around declaring their vacancy with illuminated roof lights, glowing down the avenues like a thousand cat eyes in the dark, desperately searching for the few random fares out there. Competition for passengers was vicious and we became even more like creeping tigers in the jungle, trying to snap up our prey before the other guy got to it. The same thing always happened during the slow months of summer, too, when many New Yorkers fled town and the tourists flocked to less oppressively humid climes.

I had been in a weird mood lately. Allie had gotten a job as a junior writer on a cable TV series and had moved out to Los Angeles for ten months. She had to quit her job teaching cartooning at the New School so she could get flown to the West Coast and make tons of money.

I was happy for her but this wasn't easy for me. Over the seven years we'd known each other, Allie and I had developed an intensely close and intimate friendship. We had our own little language and everyone always thought of us as sisters. One Halloween, we decided to dress up as conjoined twins. Squeezed together into a giant Hanson T-shirt and wearing matching red baseball hats, we walked up Sixth Avenue in the Halloween parade holding a sign that said AS GOD MADE US. This was our friendship in a nutshell.

We were perfectly and, sometimes, brutally honest with each other. If my hair looked bad, I knew Allie would be the only one who would tell me. If she said something stupid to a girl she liked, I would let her know. But it worked both ways, and when I thought she did something well, like a paper she was writing or a comic she was working on, she knew I wasn't lying or protecting her feelings by telling her it was good.

Allie was my anchor, and when I started to spin out, which happened every so often, she was the only one who could reel me back in and talk me down. At some point along the way we half jokingly declared ourselves "nonsexual life partners." Hanging on my wall is a one-page comic she drew for my birthday. In it, each panel represents a year of our friendship. The final panel shows our tombstones placed side by side in the year 2070. On both stones, under our names, are the words DAUGHTER, MOTHER, WIFE, NONSEXUAL LIFE PARTNER.

I took Allie to the airport in the middle of January, and when she was gone, I felt left behind. Things were sort of gloomy and lonely those days.

She called me the day after she got to California and left a message describing how she was walking along Venice Beach watching the Rollerbladers and the bodybuilders, how there were bubbles blowing in the wind and handsome lovers strolling on the boardwalk. She was wearing short sleeves and sunglasses and eating seared tuna for lunch. I, meanwhile, was wearing thermal underwear in my cab with the heat blasting, trying not to skid out on the ice, and eating peanuts out of a can that I kept on the floor in front of the passenger seat.

I had also picked up the weird habit of speaking out loud to myself when alone in the cab, especially when it was slow. I would find myself late at night on an empty street, devoid of pedestrians and street hails, and I would put on a fake British accent and say, "Excuse me, sir, would you like a taxi?"

Sometimes it felt like I was going a little crazy. My trajectory couldn't have been more different from Allie's. She was on her way to big success, making more money than either of us could even comprehend, while I was driving this cab in New York, earning a living in forty-cent increments.

I was starting to feel a little stuck, starting to question where exactly all this was going. When would I get my fill of this adventure? Where was it going to lead me? What did I actually want from all this to begin with? And had it happened yet and I just didn't know it? I was worried that this was it. Some part of me was convinced that I needed to do this for at least a year before I moved on, but what was next? I didn't know.

What I did know was that I definitely didn't want to be driving a cab for the rest of my life. The novelty of it was already wearing off, but I couldn't stop yet. I couldn't stop even if I wanted to at that point because I had no other immediate way of making money. Also, I was still determined to see the adventure through, no matter what happened along the way. I just didn't know when, exactly, it would be time to stop.

Allie was gone and I was in New York and, despite the other friends I had around, I felt alone.

It was yet another slow day in late January and I had just started my shift when I was flagged down by a forty-something-year-old blond lady. She was accompanied by a very old man in a wheelchair, so I popped the trunk and got out to help. The woman was trying to load the guy into the backseat, and as I tried to assist her, she refused my help, saying she could do it on her own.

I figured she knew what she was doing so I stood there in the cold and watched as she dumped the guy onto the floor in the back and slammed the door. I began folding up the wheelchair to fit it into the trunk and she looked at me and said, "You must be an angel." She kept repeating this over and over again as I struggled with the wheelchair.

At that moment, Harvey happened to drive by and saw me in this situation. He rolled down his window and, laughing a little, said, "Good luck with that wheelchair!" before driving off with a grin.

When I finally got back into the cab, the woman had situated herself in the back and continued telling me what an "angel" I was. The man was stuck on the floor, his body wedged between the backseat and the partition, and he was none too happy about it. He started screaming and cursing at her, saying, "You fucking motherfucking bitch. Look at me! Get

HACK

off127

me off the floor, you rancid bitch." To which she kept calmly saying, "It's okay, honey, don't worry about it. Everything's fine."

She continued brushing off his insults and proceeded to tell me that she had just won $600 playing a scratch-off lotto card and that they had been celebrating with some drinks. The man on the floor kept screaming at her, saying stuff like, "You're not gonna get any of my money, you filthy whore! It's OVER! I hate you!"

She leaned up to the front and said to me, "He's a millionaire, and you must be an angel."

They were going to Tudor City and we of course got stuck in rush-hour traffic down Second Avenue. The man continued his tirade for the entire trip, which, though somewhat amusing, also made it a little stressful.

Him: "I can't stand you. It's over, you fucking bitch. This is insane!"

Her: "Honey, it's fine. You know you love me. Sometimes insanity is the best policy."

When we finally got to the corner of 41st and Second, she told me to stop. She got out and tried to pick the old man up off the floor of the cab, but couldn't do it. I got out to help, but he was too heavy and we were too weak. I had set the wheelchair next to the door, but we had the guy only half out of the cab when she said, "There's a liquor store up the street." (Of course she knew where *that* was.) "I'll go ask the man who works there to help."

She left me alone holding the man under the armpits. I continued to try to get him out, and managed to pull him fully out of the cab, but now his legs were *under* the cab resting limply in the street slush, and I couldn't lift him up anymore. I was beginning to panic, so I looked around and spotted a middle-aged guy in a suit walking past. I called over and asked him for help.

Seeing the situation, he kindly walked over, grabbed the guy's legs, and together we hoisted him into the chair.

As this Good Samaritan was walking away, the woman came back from the liquor store accompanied by an embarrassed-looking young man. She stood there staring dumbly at me and repeated yet again that I must be an angel. Then she held up a twenty-dollar bill and said, "Did I pay you already?" I told her she had, and she paused for a second before handing me the twenty anyway, which I totally deserved.

The old man politely thanked me and then resumed cursing and screaming at the woman as she wheeled him away up the street.

When I showed up at the garage on Super Bowl Sunday, Ricky was in full form. He smelled worse than usual, if that's possible, which drove most of the guys out of the waiting room. Usually they tolerated it somehow, but I couldn't stomach it and always stayed as far away as I could.

When Ricky saw me, he made sure to let me know he had placed a $50 bet on one of the teams playing in the big game that night. Then he rambled on for a while about football before asking me to unlock the women's bathroom for him.

I'm not sure why he always insisted on using the women's bathroom, since the men's room couldn't possibly smell bad to him, but I usually opened it for him when he asked. This time, though, I had to say no since I knew I was going to have to go in there before I started my shift, and his smell was so bad this day, it was just going to linger in there and quite possibly make me vomit.

When I said no, I tried to just rush past him so he couldn't ask me why or make me feel bad, but before I got out of the waiting room, he told me once again, for about the hundredth time, "You're gonna be here for thirty years, Melissa."

I said, "I hope not," and walked out.

A little while later, when I got my cab, it had the faint smell of urine. The mark of Ricky. He must've driven that particular cab a few nights before, but fortunately, enough time had passed and the smell wasn't too strong. I scrubbed down the inside of the cab with bleach wipes and pulled out with all the windows down, despite the freezing cold air outside. I was able to kill off the smell for the most part and make it manageable.

I expected the night's rhythm to be off because of the Super Bowl, so I mentally prepared myself for a quiet four hours while the game was on. Sure enough, there was a mad rush before the game, with everyone going to parties and sports bars, and then around 6:30, traffic thinned out and there were only a few stray pedestrians on the sidewalks.

Neither of the teams playing were from New York, and most people were pretty indifferent about the game itself, but they were all going to sit through the parties anyway. When it ended, there was another burst of business, and then by 1:30, the city was quiet again. I was tired and ready to go home so I called it a night.

When I pulled into the garage, Ricky was already back. Oddly, his smell was less pungent than it had been earlier. This time when he saw me, he said, "I blame you for making me lose the Super Bowl, Melissa. I lost fifty dollars."

I guess he bet on the wrong team.

By that time, my friendships at the garage had solidified and I had a little clique of guys I always hung around with when I was there. I was much more comfortable, didn't get stared at as much anymore, and I felt accepted and normal. The guys spoke frankly in front of me and didn't treat me any differently when telling a story, though occasionally one of them would apologize for cursing in my presence. I don't know why they thought my ears were so fucking delicate, but whatever.

A few weeks into February, Harvey and I had an "important

conversation." I walked into the garage, and when he saw me, he said, "Melissa, I'd like to talk to you. Come outside with me a second."

I followed him out into the yard and he said, "I wanted to tell you, you and I have something in common."

I replied, "Okay. . . . What is it?" I had no idea what he was going to say. I thought, *Maybe he actually is gay and wants to come out to me.* I wasn't particularly "out" at the garage, so I didn't really know if he read me as gay or not. Daniel knew, but I don't know if anyone else did, and it didn't really matter to me much.

Instead, he said, "In my *other* persona, my middle name is Melissa."

I was a little confused. "Huh?"

He said, "Outside of the garage, I go by Helen. Melissa is my middle name. So instead of Harvey Melvin, I'm Helen Melissa. I've changed my bank account to say H. M. Kortmansky, so that it's all gender-neutral."

It seemed as if he had been preparing to tell me this for a while and had decided that today was the day. I realized he wanted me to know him, and I guess he finally felt comfortable coming out to me.

I replied, "So you're transsexual?"

He said, "I prefer the term 'transgendered.'"

"Okay. But why are you telling me this? How did you know I was gay?"

His face registered the tiniest smile of surprise as he said, "Oh! I didn't. Until right now. I just thought you might understand. I find it easier to talk to women."

"So do you, like, date guys?"

He answered, "No, I'm a lesbian."

I guess Paul and Martin had it right, even though they couldn't have been more wrong. Harvey wasn't gay, but Helen *was.*

I don't know why I was surprised. Quite a few people in the queer scene that I hung out in had transitioned, but most of them had gone from being female to male.

Helen, on the other hand, was a little different. She was sixty-two years old, had never taken female hormones, and just didn't pass for a woman at all. It was a little bit more difficult for me to accept. I mean, I *accepted* it, I just found it a little hard to adjust my thinking. She looked like a man in women's clothing, she had the deepest voice ever, and she had an ex-wife and two grown daughters. But she was also from a different generation of queers, with not too many options available to her for most of her life.

The young transsexuals I knew had so many more opportunities. They had slightly easier access to hormones, surgeries, and the rest of the stuff that went into transitioning from one sex to another. It was simply easier for them to eventually fit into the world. Things had loosened up quite a bit since Helen's youth, and straight society, though still not perfect, was much more accepting than it had ever been before. But, frankly, it was just much easier to go from female to male than the other way around.

"So should I call you Helen from now on?" I asked.

"Well, around here you should continue calling me Harvey. These guys are all a bunch of lunatics. Their heads might explode if they heard you calling me Helen. But, yes, when we talk on the phone, or if we ever spend time outside of the garage—which I hope we'll soon do—call me Helen."

She continued, "And while we're on the subject, I'd like to get your phone number."

We traded numbers, but I already had a "Helen" in my phone book, so I entered her in as "Helen Harvey," where she remains to this day.

I called Allie in California to tell her of this newest development. She had recently dated a very outspoken male-to-female transsexual who I, incidentally, had hated, but that's neither here nor there. I told her about Helen and said, "But it's sad because she really doesn't pass, like, at all. She just looks like a man in women's clothing. Most people think she's a crossdresser or some kind of freak. She talked about wanting to go on hormones, but what difference can that really make?"

Allie spoke with a tone of authority. "Well, it'll change her muscle tone and she'll develop breasts eventually, but her voice will never get higher. Estrogen doesn't work on the voice the same way testosterone does." I already knew this, but since she'd met that last girlfriend, Allie thought of herself as sort of an expert on transsexuality. It had become an "issue" she all of a sudden cared deeply about. And the truth was, she *did* know more about it than me. I knew a thing or two about the female-to-male transition, but not so much the other way around.

I didn't really even know what I wanted Allie to tell me. We both knew that life would be hard for Helen. She was too old to pass, her voice too deep. It pained me that there was nothing I could do to make her life easier, so I was determined to simply be respectful of her choice and always treat her the way she wanted to be treated, to always use female pronouns when we talked in private, to always call her Helen, to make her feel the way she wanted to feel.

It's not like she wasn't tough or that she even needed my protection or help, though my first instinct was to give it. She was strong as hell, and it was no small thing that she dressed the way she did and showed up at the garage, got into a cab, and drove the streets that way. Helen took a lot of shit, but she didn't care. Or she didn't seem to, at least. She was proud and sure of herself, and ultimately, I guess that's all that mattered.

This whole business made me see her in a new light. She somehow became more real to me. She was doing something that took a shitload of guts, more guts than I ever thought I could have. She couldn't bear living in the world the way she was born, so she lived in it the way she wanted, and tried as hard as she could to make it adapt to her image of herself, as impossible as that seemed. When Harvey became Helen, we became friends. An unlikely pair, to be sure—me and this sixty-two-year-old transgendered cab driver—but friends nonetheless.

CHAPTER 12

The bitter weather seemed to bring out the drunks and the crazies. Or maybe it forced all the relatively sane people indoors, leaving only the oblivious weirdos on the streets. Either way, I had a string of them in my cab over the next few weeks. I guess I was fortunate that no one did anything truly insane in the cab, but I knew there was trouble when people got in and couldn't—or wouldn't—tell me where to go.

The first time this happened was when I picked up a very drunk yuppified white guy on Lexington Avenue. He was able to tell me he wanted to go to South Orange, New Jersey, but that was it. After that, communication between us deteriorated.

The way we deal with out-of-city fares is to either double the meter from the city line or negotiate with the passenger on a flat rate, including the tolls. Either way, the price is supposed to compensate for the fact that we cannot, by law, pick up a passenger outside of New York City, which means we'll be driving the entire distance back empty.

I have to admit that, at the time, I was severely prejudiced against the entire state of New Jersey. This was not only because I found their roads too confusing and because you had to cross an inconvenient bridge or tunnel to get there, but also because of the massive rivalry between New York drivers and those from Jersey. Of course, this wasn't unique to New York and New Jersey. It seemed pretty evident that drivers from every nearby state despised the drivers from whichever states were their closest neighbors. So New York drivers hated New Jersey and Connecticut drivers, New Jersey drivers hated New York and Pennsylvania drivers, Pennsylvania drivers hated New Jersey and probably drivers from Ohio, and so on.

I had decided by then, perhaps unjustly so, that New Jersey drivers were the worst of the worst because they didn't seem to know how to drive properly in New York City. I had seen too many cars with Jersey plates neglect to use their turn signals, make right turns on red (which is illegal in NYC), and drive with an incredible sense of entitlement. And they were *always* on the phone. Admittedly, plenty of drivers from New York did the exact same things, but when it was coupled with that pale yellow license plate with THE GARDEN STATE emblazoned across the bottom, it only fueled my prejudices.

I had also made the determination that the worst cars on the road were white Mercedes SUVs with Jersey plates. Each of these characteristics stood alone as a sign that the person would drive like an asshole, but put them together and you got the shittiest drivers ever. They were the ones who would dangerously cut you off, forcing you to slam on your brakes or swerve into oncoming traffic, and then, to add insult to injury, they would give you the finger because you honked.

Still, going out of town meant good money, so I took the job, despite the fact that the guy was clearly wasted. The first thing he slurred when he jumped in was, "So where are we going?" A red flag went up immediately.

I was like, "Uh, I think *you're* supposed to tell *me* that."

He replied, "Right, right. South Orange."

"Jersey?"

"Yeah, New Jersey."

I said, "Okay, I need to check the out-of-town fare book for the rate," but before I could find a price, he said, "It's a hundred dollars."

I had just gotten to the page where it said the fare was $90, so I said, "Yeah, I guess that'll work. But we have to add on for the tolls as we go. Can you direct me there?"

It had been another slow night. Seeing how drunk he was, I probably should've just kicked him out, but as long as he had the money, I wasn't going to care. He assured me that he could direct me, since I wasn't so sharp on how to get around once outside the city.

As we started across town toward the Lincoln Tunnel, I remembered the first time I had to take a fare somewhere that I needed directions for. My passenger had just flown in from Seattle and needed to go to the Bronx Zoo. I'd picked him up at LaGuardia and, since I had waited there for over an hour, I didn't want to refuse the job. He had flown in for a conservationists' convention at the zoo and was being put up at some apartments they had on the premises. He'd never been to New York before, so he was no help directions-wise.

It was 5:30 P.M. and, since I wasn't sure what the correct

route was, I made the mistake of calling my mom. She and my stepfather both grew up in the Bronx and knew their way around that borough better than they knew how to get around Rockland County, where they currently lived.

When she picked up the phone, I said, "Mom, listen, I need directions to the Bronx Zoo from LaGuardia. I'm heading toward the Triborough Bridge right now. What do I do after that?"

But instead of just telling me, she said, in her Jewish-mother way, "What are you going to the zoo for? It's five-thirty! Isn't the zoo closed?"

Exasperated, I just said, "Mom, that's not important right now. I have a passenger and that's where he wants to go. Can you just tell me how to get there? I'm on the bridge already now."

She said, "Hold on," and then I heard her in the background calling for my stepfather to pick up the extension. When he got on the line, she told him, "Melissa needs directions to the Bronx Zoo. She's on the Triborough Bridge."

Hearing this, my stepfather said, "What does she want to go to the zoo for? Isn't the zoo closed?"

I barked something about how I needed to know NOW, no time to explain, and he finally gave me a viable route. It was an important lesson, though, that I should never call my parents for directions if I don't have time for the meddling commentary.

But this night, I didn't even have the option of calling my mom, or anyone else for that matter. It was late, and besides, she definitely didn't know how to direct me to South Orange, New Jersey. I had to rely on my passenger, which would have been fine, except he was on the incoherent side of the spectrum.

When we got through the Lincoln Tunnel, he was so out of it, he couldn't tell me where to go. Actually, he *wouldn't* tell me where to go. He was being stupid and annoying and treating me like we had some sort of relationship happening between us other than driver-passenger.

There were signs for different exits and I needed to make a choice, and quick. But when I asked him which highway to take, all he kept saying was, "Why do you hate me? No, really. Why do you hate me?"

I said, "I don't hate you. In fact, I don't care about you one way or the other. I just want you to tell me where to turn so I can take you where you want to go."

Ignoring the fact that I was, at that point, taking the wrong exit, he replied, "My ex-girlfriend hates me. She doesn't understand. She's such a bitch. Why do you hate me?"

My patience was being tested and I was getting angry. I kept asking for directions and he kept talking about his ex and asking why I hated him. After five more minutes of this, and of driving aimlessly on random New Jersey highways, I snapped. We were on a straightaway and I turned around and yelled.

"I am WORKING. This is my JOB. I don't hate you, though I will start to pretty soon if you don't tell me where to go. Cut the shit NOW and tell me where the fuck to go!"

He quieted down for a second and said, "Exit here." I don't even think he knew where we were or which exit we were at, but I got off the highway anyway, figuring, if anything, I'd find a gas station and ask for directions.

I pulled into an Exxon. When I stopped the cab, yuppie guy got out and said, "I gotta take a piss," and walked off to use the bathroom like he thought we were on some sort of road trip together and this was just a fun little rest stop for coffee and bathroom breaks and souvenir shopping.

The guys in the gas station were completely unhelpful but they had maps for sale, so I flipped through one of them and found a route that looked sort of right. We got back into the cab and continued on, with me stopping other drivers to confirm my directions just in case. The last thing I wanted was to stay lost in New Jersey with this guy.

The whole rest of the ride, I had to deflect his pathetic questioning of why I hated him, and other drunken blathering. After twenty-five more minutes of this, I finally found his house.

He handed me a $100 bill and said, "Do you want a tip?" Like I'm gonna say no.

"Sure, a tip would be nice." I certainly deserved one after dealing with all his bullshit. He handed me a $20 bill and said, "I know you hate me, but here's my card." He handed me a business card that said he was a banker and worked at Deutsche Bank.

Gee, thanks, because I was totally hoping we could keep in touch.

I seemed to be getting sick a lot. Too often, in fact. My muscles were always tense and I occasionally woke up in full neck spasm, unable to move or turn my head. No amount of ibuprofin or painkillers could get me behind the wheel safely and without total misery, so I would be forced to stay home.

Other times it was my knees and legs and even my feet that caused me trouble. And sometimes it was a package deal involving my back, shoulders, arms, and hands. And, probably because it was winter, I also seemed to be getting a cold or the flu about once a month.

It was always something. I mean, I was never the healthiest person in the world to begin with and, when it came to diet, I certainly ate for shit. Not to mention that I smoked too much. But I seemed to be getting more sick more often, and with a whole new potpourri of problems.

Headaches, arm cramps, kidney pains, eye twitches, and so on. I knew it was from driving. It had to be. From the prolonged sitting; from the hard gripping of the wheel over the course of a twelve-hour shift; from repeatedly pumping the gas and brake with my right leg (and, eventually, my left leg too); from not peeing as often as I should; from touching dirty, germ-infested money all night long. From not sleeping enough, and from getting extreme rushes of adrenaline at least three or four times a night, and from having no outlet for it other than my stationary muscles.

And probably most of all, from the stress. The stress of traffic, of near-accidents, of money worries, of asshole passengers. Of the whole damn thing. I just wasn't physically strong enough to manage it.

So, after having been out sick again for a week, I returned to the cab just in time to meet another difficult passenger. Eager to get a jump on the shift and to get back into some kind of rhythm, I showed up at the garage earlier than usual. Paul the crazy Romanian dispatcher told me I was too early and I wasn't going to get a cab for at least two hours. In fact, I waited nearly three hours.

When I finally got out, I headed for the lower level of the 59th Street Bridge. On my approach, at 41st Avenue and Crescent Street in Queens, an old grizzled white man hopped into the back as I was stopped at a red light. When he got in, I asked, "Where to?" I already knew from my earlier experiences with men of his type that he was trouble, but he had gotten in without me seeing him, and now that he was in, I had no power to refuse him.

His scowled response only confirmed my suspicions. "I don't have to tell you where I'm going. Just go."

At first I thought he was kidding. I said, "Okay . . . do you want me to go over the bridge?" because I wasn't sure if he wanted to go somewhere in Queens or Manhattan. He replied, "No, I want you to go *under* the bridge. Let me see you do *that*."

I didn't really know what to do at that point, so when I got to the light at which I would either continue onto the bridge or turn to avoid it and stay in Queens, I said, "You really need to tell me where you want to go."

He started arguing with me, reminding me that it was none of my business where he wanted to go, until, not in the mood for this at all, I finally snapped and said, "Do I need to get the cops?" Because at that point I was convinced he was just fucking crazy.

"Don't try to threaten me with the cops. You got nothin' on me," he answered. I was so perplexed, I just sat there gaping at him. Something must've clicked in that unkempt head of his because the next moment he said, "Oh, right, right, right. The TLC changed the law. I forgot about that. Fine, fine. Fifty-first Street and Second Avenue. I apologize. Let's not fight."

I got on the bridge, relieved that he was actually going somewhere and hadn't just gotten into my cab for no reason other than he was crazy and had nothing else to do. The rest of the ride was uneventful, and he even tipped me a dollar in the end.

As he was getting out, perhaps just to punctuate our time together, he remarked, "I will say this, you're a good driver." Then he popped his head back in and cheerfully added, "Be safe, and don't kill any kittens!"

One Wednesday night in early March, another strange man got into my cab on Steinway Street in Queens. I was sitting at a red light when I noticed a guy standing around the corner with his arm up, hailing me. I only saw him at the last second so I sort of jumped over a bit to make the right turn when the light changed.

What I didn't realize was that there was a car a little behind me on my right side, exactly in my blind spot. What I also didn't realize until I stopped short just in time to avoid colliding with it was that it was a cop car. My head filled with only one thought: *Fuck*.

We both just sat still for a minute, and when I realized they weren't going to move, I continued making the turn, then stopped on the corner, rolled down my window, and waited.

When they pulled up next to me, I saw the driver was a young male cop and his partner in the passenger seat was a youngish woman cop with long blond hair. She just looked at me expectantly, so I said, "I'm really sorry about that. I didn't even see you there." She replied sternly, "Well, you better start being more aware. You should look next time."

I didn't really want to argue and explain that I *had* looked but that they were in my blind spot and, not only that, I happened to pride myself on being a pretty aware driver, if I may say so myself. So instead I just said, "Okay, yeah. Sorry."

At that point, the male cop, who looked like he was just barely holding himself back, let loose and yelled at the top of his lungs, "You guys all drive like FUCKING SHIT!"

This pissed me off. I wanted to yell something back, something obnoxious like "And you don't?" but I knew that was the absolute wrong move, so I just squinted my eyes and kept my mouth shut. This guy could do what he wanted with me and there wasn't a damn thing I could do about it. But I could tell the female cop was willing to just let the whole thing go. I could also tell she was the only thing holding her partner back from making my life hell.

Meanwhile, the guy who had hailed me got into the cab, opened his window, and said to the cops, "I'd rather go with you guys than with her." I had no idea where this was coming from, and if he was saying that, why the hell was he getting into the cab anyway?

The cops read his comment a little differently. It put them on alert and I could tell they were wondering now if maybe there wasn't something fishy about this guy. They said, "What do you mean?" He just lazily replied, "I'd just rather go with someone who's more . . . sober, I guess."

I realized he was trying to make a joke, trying to make friends with the little police people and clearly thought himself very clever. No one laughed. And when the lady cop saw what I was going to have to deal with for the next however many minutes, I'm pretty sure she felt bad for me.

She stared at him blankly and said, "Trust me, you *don't* want to come with us." Then she gave me an almost sympathetic look, told me to be careful one more time, and they pulled away.

I was about to say something to the guy about how fucked up that was, but he stopped me by saying, "Cops. They have no sense of humor." I couldn't really argue with that, so I just said, "I'm sober. I don't know why you just said that to them. Are you trying to get me into trouble or something?"

He replied, "I don't know why I said that either. *I'm* the one who's drunk."

I already knew this guy was bad news and I considered kicking him out of the cab then and there, but instead I found myself asking him where he wanted to go. I figured, *Let's just get this over with.* He said, "Fifty-first Street and Queens Boulevard."

Queens is a huge borough and it's not the easiest place to navigate. Usually if someone's going somewhere in Queens, they know the best way to get there, so I just ask them for directions. Sure, I could find it on my map eventually and figure it out, but it's easier if they can tell me.

I said, "Can you direct me there?"

He said, "Yeah, make a right."

I knew enough about where I was to know that this was the wrong way, but I went with it, figuring he was taking some secret roundabout route I didn't know about. I realized something was up, though, when he just kept telling me to turn right every couple of blocks so that we were going in widening circles like in that Winnie-the-Pooh story where they keep coming back to the same spot no matter which direction they set out in.

I started to get even more irritated with this guy, but I was still treating him like a normal person, which, I realized later, was the wrong move. He apparently *needed* to be a little bit abused, but that's a whole different profession, and one that pays more, to boot.

I said, "Okay, we keep making circles and you keep telling me to go in the opposite direction of your destination. I think we should go *left* here, not right."

He replied, "*I'm* the boss here. *I'm* paying *you.* I'll tell you where to go. And besides, I shouldn't have to direct you. You should know your way around." Oh, so he wanted to play like that? Okay, fine.

I said, "Guess what? You haven't paid me yet, you're *not* my boss, and if you don't like how I'm doing my job, you're welcome to get the fuck out right here." I stopped the cab.

This made him back off a little. He said, "I'm just kidding! God, you need to lighten up. I think I just want to drive around with you for a while. You have a good New York accent." He dug a $20 bill out of his pocket and handed it to me through the partition. "Here, just drive around until this runs out."

I was in no position to say no to cash. Plus, I was relieved he even had money on him after all, since him beating the fare would have almost been an appropriate end to the trip. So we drove, and he kept arbitrarily telling me to turn right.

Then he started in on me, saying, "You know, you really need to hold out for the day shift. You shouldn't be driving at night. Aren't you scared of me?" When I answered that I was not, he was disappointed, saying, "Aren't I intimidating at *all*?"

Again, I said no. I really wasn't scared. Annoyed and a little pissed off maybe, but definitely not scared.

Then he said, "Okay, fine. I've changed my mind. I'm not going home. I'm going to a strip club. Wanna come?" I said,

"No, thank you." He said, "Fine, you can drop me off at the strip club and then go find all those frat boys you didn't meet in college." And after a pause, he thought he'd give it another shot, "Unless you want to park and come in with me."

I got him to give me the address of the strip club and headed in that direction, not giving a shit if the meter came to $20. I ignored his directions and just went the way I knew was right until we finally got a block from the club. He told me to stop there and said, "Okay, now you can park and come in with me." Again, I refused.

The meter was at $17. He said, "Is three dollars a good tip?" I answered, "After what you just put me through, no. It's not." He looked at me for a second, considering. Then he said, "You have the best sense of humor of any cabbie ever." He handed over another $20 and said, "Come back for me in a little while and I'll tell you how the strippers were."

I smiled and sarcastically said, "Sure, I'll be sure to swing by in a little while." When he finally got out, I headed toward the 59th Street Bridge and back to the civilized world.

I was sitting at the light at Bank and Hudson in the West Village when a late-middle-aged lady hopped in. She was sweet and weird and oddly mannered, and she told me she was going to her mother's house on East Houston Street. She said she took care of her mother a lot and that it was hard and sometimes they didn't really get along.

Somehow the conversation turned to television and, I'm not sure why, I told her how on *The Sopranos,* the Tony character had to take care of his mom for a while even though she had plotted to have him killed. The woman responded, "Oh, I don't really watch too many shows anymore. I only watch the shopping channels."

She listed off all the different shopping networks, such as

QVC, ShopNBC, HSN, etc., and described the merits and drawbacks of each one.

When I asked her how much money she spent on home shopping, she said, "Oh no, no, no, I don't buy anything anymore. I just watch. I *used* to buy from them, though. Ten years ago I drained a bank account—and it was a *good* bank account too, you should've seen it—but I don't do that anymore. Now I just watch them."

The way she spoke was so gentle, almost timid, and she kept cutting herself off and starting new sentences in the middle of other sentences. I felt sorry for her. It was like she felt that these shopping channels spoke directly to her, kept her company and warded off loneliness. The schlocky hosts were the closest things she had to friends or something, which made sense when she mentioned that her husband was, after all, a Bush-voting, NRA-card-carrying Republican who ignored her.

I felt nothing but fondness and affection for this poor woman. She was so utterly sweet, and clearly had a few problems, but she fell into a category of crazy that only made her more endearing. Unlike all the other unstable people I'd had in my cab, who somehow found a way to include me in their problems, this woman just needed someone to talk to. I was happy to be that person for a few minutes as I ferried her to her mother's house, where she was planning on spending the night doing her mom's chores and hanging out with her "friends" on the TV.

C H A P T E R   1 3

Winter seemed to be lasting forever and the job was wearing me down. I was getting sick more and more, and my body was beaten by the cold weather, the long hours sitting behind the wheel, and the stress. I was calling out of work on a regular basis. I just didn't want to go anymore. All I wanted was to stay inside my apartment reading, playing video games, and annoying my fat lazy cats out of their naps. I wanted to insulate myself from the all-too-real world outside.

On top of the head colds and flus, my knees were getting

stiff and rickety, my back seemed to spend half its life in spasm, and my left foot was being an asshole. The foot in particular had been a problem ever since it got broken when I got hit by a car a year and a half before, as I was jaywalking across 23rd Street. I was still waiting on a settlement from the accident and it wasn't coming soon enough. I desperately wanted a break, a paid vacation.

My temper was also spinning even more out of control and I was getting into more fights and arguments, mainly with other cabbies.

On one particularly long disjointed night, I got into a screaming match with another cabbie who had pulled a really fucked-up move that forced me into oncoming traffic.

We were both making the left turn from 11th Avenue onto 23rd Street. There were two turn lanes so that two cars could turn at the same time as long as they followed the lines and stayed in the lane they were turning from.

I was in the left lane and the other cabbie was in the right. But as he made the turn, he cut over into my lane on 23rd, where I was supposed to be, thus making me swerve onto the wrong side of the street to avoid getting hit by him. Luckily, there were no cars coming and I was able to fall back in time. He must've seen this happen, because when I pulled next to him after he finally moved back into the right lane, he rolled his window down and started yelling at me as sort of a preemptive defense. Of course, he believed very strongly that he'd done absolutely nothing wrong and that I was the asshole for trying to turn next to him.

I started yelling back, and we drove side by side for a minute just screaming like maniacs at each other. He said, "You have problem? What's wrong with you?" He was just *so* innocent.

I called out, "I wouldn't have a problem if you learned how to fucking drive!"

"Suck my dick!"

Typical. He even pointed to the area in case I didn't know where exactly his dick might reside.

I yelled back, "I would if you had one, but since you don't, *you* can suck *mine!*"

I couldn't tell if he was confused or offended, but right after that, he turned down Ninth Avenue while I got hailed and picked up my next passenger. Either way, I considered it a victory.

Later that same week, a cabbie punched my driver-side window. I wouldn't let him cut in front of me from the far left lane on 33rd Street going toward Penn Station, and I guess that really bothered him. In my rearview, I saw him get out of his cab as we were stopped at the light, so I locked my doors and put my windows up.

He came up to my cab and started yelling at me, but I just ignored him and casually waved him away, as if he were an insignificant little mosquito. I guess that bothered him even more because that's when he punched the window.

It didn't break or crack or anything, but it served to trigger my temper in a bad way. I was sure he would not have done that if I was a guy, but I'm not, so he felt perfectly safe acting like such a reckless dick.

I was so enraged, I grabbed my little camera that I'd recently started carrying around with me and flung my door open, saying, "You wanna hit me? Go the fuck ahead! I'm right here. What the fuck are you gonna do now?"

As stupid a move as that may sound, I felt pretty sure he wouldn't do anything and I wanted to call his bluff. It was just so outrageous that he thought he could bully me and get away with it, like I would be scared of him or something. By that point, it wasn't easy to intimidate me. I had seen enough to just know that being scared of jerks like this was a waste of energy. What I hadn't realized yet was that getting angry at them was also a waste of energy. So I let my anger run free and, you know what? It felt damn good. Of course, when this guy was confronted with my boiling rage and insanity, not to mention my camera, he quickly backed off and ran back to his cab.

When I told my next passengers about the incident, they relayed a story about a fight they once witnessed between two cabbies. They had been trying to hail a cab and two pulled up and crashed into each other in their attempt to try to claim them as passengers. Both drivers apparently got out and started yelling at each other and kicking each other's cabs. In the meantime, the passengers flagged down a third cab, got in, and left the scene.

We were discussing all the different kinds of arguments and fights that happen on the streets, when one of them said to me, "I'm surprised you guys don't carry guns."

I replied, "If we had guns, there wouldn't be anyone left in this city."

I never considered myself a violent person, but I can definitely recount some murderous rages I experienced while driving the cab, and I do think if I'd had a weapon, it would've been hard to resist using it. I don't think I'm alone in that either.

Later that night, at around 1:30 A.M.—so I guess it counts as morning actually—my new friend from the garage, Rodrigo, offered to buy me dinner at a kebob house on MacDougal Street. It had been a slow night, but he was having an excellent shift. He called it "the Rodrigo luck." And it was funny because he always did seem to somehow get great fares when everyone else was searching and suffering. Then he would send me text messages about it, making sure to mention the awesome amount of money he'd made, just to tease me. I would usually text something back along the lines of "Fuck you" because I was so jealous.

But that night, he wanted to spread the wealth in the form of dinner. He bought me a shish kebob and we stood on the street and ate. I told him about the guy who punched my window, and Rodrigo, a big Puerto Rican guy, agreed with me, saying, "Yeah, if he saw *me* behind the wheel, he would not have done that."

I went back to the garage early that night because the city was a ghost town with thousands of empty cabs haunting every street. It's funny how philosophical cabbies get when they make an extra shitty amount of money for the hours they put in on their shift.

That night back at the garage, I heard them saying little makeshift maxims like, "There are good nights, and then sometimes there are just nights," and, "Another day, another dollar. Except for the dollar part."

I was glad the night was over.

The near-death experiences were starting to blend together, so that when it became too near for me to tolerate, my rage just snowballed into a disproportionately large fury. Again, it was another cabbie, and he pulled a stupid move that put me and my passengers in danger.

The cabbie in question had dangerously cut me off just to sit in front of me at the next red light. And, to make it an even more useless move, we both had passengers, so it wasn't even like we were competing for a fare, which would've made more sense. Instead, it was just pointless and ridiculous.

We were on 14th Street, which has two lanes going in each direction, and after the offending move, the cabbie pulled into the middle of both lanes to prevent me from pulling up next to him and chewing him out. When we stopped at the light, I got out of my cab, leaving my young passengers alone in the back. I very calmly walked up to his window, which was closed, hacked up all the phlegm I could muster, and spit on it.

His passengers looked shocked. And so did he, for that matter. That was all I needed. What else could I do?

I walked back to my cab and casually resettled into my seat. My passengers said, "What did you just do?"

I answered, "I spit on his window."

They said, "You rule! That is so awesome!"

I was happy and proud, I had new allies, and the rest of the ride was fun. When they got out, they tipped me generously and said, "You are the best cab driver ever."

Unfortunately, this type of hair-trigger behavior was spreading out into my non-cab life. I was hanging out at a friend's apartment, which was located on the Disney-fied block of St. Marks Place between Second and Third Avenues, and we left her building to go rent a video. We stood in the middle of the block, just off the curb, waiting for the cars to pass so we could cross the street.

I was looking to my right, watching the last few cars come up the block, when all of a sudden I got bodychecked from behind and was sent lurching forward into the path of an oncoming car. Luckily the driver was able to respond quickly enough to swerve out of the way and avoid hitting me.

At first, I thought my friend was being a stupid idiot by knocking into me, or maybe she'd tripped or something, but when I turned around and realized that it was just some guy I didn't know who had needlessly and viciously pushed me into traffic, my fury was unleashed.

He continued crossing the street like he owned the whole fucking world, and I followed him. I wasn't going to let him get away with that. I started going off, first registering my disbelief, saying, "What the fuck? Why the fuck did you push me?"

He replied by saying, "Fuck off. You were looking the other way. I wanted to cross the street."

I said, "Yeah. I was looking the other way because I was waiting for the cars to pass, you fucking prick! You almost pushed me in front of one!"

I don't remember what he said after that, I was just so enraged, but I know I kept yelling at him while he kept walking away. I followed behind him and my anger only grew, until finally, I got a running start up to him, planted both hands on his back, and shoved him as hard as I could. As I was doing this, I yelled, "Just because you can push someone who's two heads shorter than you doesn't make you tough, you fucking idiot!"

There were some guys hanging out on the block who were clearly getting a kick out of the whole exchange. And frankly, I was surprised this guy didn't turn around and hit me after I pushed him, but I didn't even care at that point. The guy just took my shove and kept walking, which only made me madder.

I pushed him again but he still wouldn't turn around.

It didn't matter to me that I would lose if this guy actually decided to engage in a fight with me. I knew I would lose, knew I would probably get very hurt. I was never the strongest person in the world, but I was brimming over with an incredible, irrational rage. The adrenaline was drumming through me, and in that moment, more than anything in the world, I *wanted* the fight. I wanted to take out all my frustration and misery and anger on this one stupid asshole who had made the mistake of messing with *me*.

When we got in front of the video store, my friend pulled me inside. I was all riled up, but also a little freaked out. I had just totally lost it on some loser guy, and for what? I was only spinning more and more out of control.

Still, it felt fucking good to push him back. And that's something I couldn't do when I was driving the cab.

It was around this time that I started imagining my own death. It's also when the dreams began. Intense anxiety-filled dreams about going too fast and someone steps out into the street, or a car is stopped in front of me and I don't have enough time to stop. I hit the brakes a second too late, or sometimes the brakes just don't work, and as I'm about to make impact, my body braces itself and I jolt awake.

There were other dreams too, about waiting around at the garage for hours and hours but never getting a cab. Dreams about cabs with weird science-fiction-type implements and antennas that made them seem like monstrous devouring aliens. But, yeah, mostly dreams of crashing and dying a horrible death, with me always waking up just at the point of impact.

After each shift, I'd come home and, too tired to take a shower, I'd just scrub the hell out of my hands, washing the black dirt out from under my fingernails—the distinctly human-scented dirt that accumulates from handling money all night, from sweaty palms gripping the grimy steering wheel. I'd go to bed and close my eyes, and a million disjointed images would run through my head, like a horror movie that I couldn't pause.

I started to feel haunted by the city, by the job, and, more than anything else, by my own lack of control. The close calls were closing in, getting closer and breathing down my neck, to the point where sometimes I just wanted to get it over with. Always a big fan of self-diagnosis, I decided that I had some form of post-traumatic stress disorder.

In my waking, driving life, each close call led me to imagine what would've or could've happened had I not swerved or hit the brakes in time. I could clearly see the side of my head smashing through the driver-side window, shattering the glass. Or the dashboard crunching up into my chest, the engine swiftly separating my legs from the rest of my body. Or the clean decapitation that would result from rear-ending the flatbed truck that stopped short just in front of me.

I could even hear the sounds of each imagined accident, and somehow, that was the worst part. I imagined the violent crunch of metal and shattering glass and the wet, glutinous sound of bodily injury and death. These sounds rang in my ears on and off through each shift.

A year and a half earlier, I had been hit by a car and ended up on crutches for an entire summer. I never saw it coming. I was, in fact, looking in the other direction, with no chance of jumping out of harm's way. But when it happened, before I even *knew* it was happening, I heard it.

It wasn't too bad, just a sickeningly hollow thud of metal door panel against body. And the next thing I knew, I was lying on the ground in the middle of 23rd Street, staring with a strange sense of curiosity and calm at all the cars and trucks that had stopped just in time to avoid running me over. And in that eerie suspended moment just after impact, there was no sound at all.

Of course, none of this made me drive any differently—I still needed to make money in a stress-filled race against time—but it intensified the rage I felt with every close call that wasn't my fault. It was rare that it ever was my fault, but when it was, I was just as angry with myself, too.

Cabbie reflexes are quick and smooth. From spending so much time driving, our awareness of our own cars as well as the other cars on the street becomes finely tuned, to the point that it's almost a sixth sense. Most people accuse cabbies of driving like maniacs, and I agree it often seems that way. But most of the time, as dangerous as it may seem, the cabbie knows exactly what he's doing.

Over the previous months, I had already developed an enhanced perception of what was happening anywhere near me on the streets, as well as what was *about* to happen in my path. I had learned to trust myself and my reflexes, knew already that there was no time to think on these streets. I intuited exactly how big my cab was, how much space I had through which to move it, and how close it was to other vehicles, without even really seeing them or being consciously aware that they were there. The car became an extension of my body. I sensed what other drivers and pedestrians were going to do before they knew it themselves.

My driving had developed a style, rhythm, and cadence that got me through each shift unharmed. But sometimes I wondered if I was secretly wishing for that one big fiery crash, the one that would take all responsibility out of my life, that would put an end to this adventure.

Every now and then, worn down, stressed out, and on a dark edge, I would imagine myself stepping out of the cab and standing in the middle of the avenue in front of an oncoming bus, holding my hand up in a stop signal as a challenge to see if it could—or would—stop in time to avoid hitting me. I wanted to stare down death. I wanted to say, "Go ahead. Hit me. See if I care."

It's not like I *wanted* to die. I valued my life and I certainly didn't feel any overt suicidal tendencies, I just felt sort of *close* to death, like I had confronted it and escaped it too many times, but only in a sidelong way.

I think my recklessness, my stupid willingness to fight, was my effort to intentionally tempt fate, to confront death head-on, like an arachnophobe who eats a spider. And while all this distressed me, I had to admit to myself that, somehow, I got off on it.

A few months earlier, back in January, I'd picked up a couple down on Essex Street. They wanted to go to Williamsburg and I pulled an illegal U-turn to get to the Williamsburg Bridge. A block later, a cop was standing in the middle of the street flashing a flashlight at me and signaling for me to pull over. *Fuck, not again,* I thought. I had checked for cops before making the U-turn, but I guess I'd missed this one. Great, another goddamn ticket.

I rolled down the window as the cop approached. He shined his flashlight inside the cab, checked out my passengers, and said, "Thanks for stopping. There was a murder near here late last night and witnesses said a cab was around at the time that it happened."

I didn't say anything and let him continue. "We were wondering if you had any information about the crime."

I was mildly shocked and said, "No, I don't know anything about it. I wasn't even working last night."

He said, "Okay, I just need your license so that I can write down that we talked to you. And when you get back to your garage tonight, we'd appreciate it if you'd put the word out that anyone who has any information should call the Seventh Precinct."

When I got home that night, I did a search for it on the Internet and discovered, as the rest of the city did the next morning, that a young actress named Nicole duFresne was shot by thieves on Clinton Street after a night of partying. The story described how, when the muggers approached her, her fiancé, and her friends with a gun drawn, she said to them, "What are you gonna do, shoot us?"

Shoot her they did, and the shot killed her.

When I read this, I couldn't help but identify with her. It was exactly what I would've done. I could see myself feeling invincible, challenging anyone who dared to mess with me or my loved ones, not believing that they would actually go through with it. Somehow I had gotten away with this behavior so far, but I realized how easily it could all go wrong.

But before I knew any of this, as I pulled away from the cop and approached the Williamsburg Bridge, I found myself feeling more relieved that I hadn't gotten another ticket than I was concerned that a young girl was dead.

CHAPTER 14

There were indeed nights that went well, when there was nothing to complain or get angry about. These were the good-luck nights, or as Rodrigo insisted, the nights when I caught some of his crazy Rodrigo luck. It was like being transported to an alternate mystical universe—a softer, sweeter New York City—in which I caught all green lights, made all the right moves, found the best fares, escaped traffic jams, and avoided collisions with a grace and skill that gave me the confidence to keep going. It was like the shift was carved out of the night just for me. My cab was the star of the city, celebrated and applauded by drivers and passengers alike. Each fare would be happy to see me and grateful for the nice swift ride. I'd find that mystical slipstream where the small obstacles didn't bother me so much and I could relax and laugh and share a surreally intimate moment with a stranger.

It was those rare beautiful moments, those even more elusive great nights when the luck was with me and the cosmos were orchestrating in my favor, that made all the sweat and the struggle, all the harrowing scares and all the crushing heartbreak, seem almost worth it. I was tapped in, even while being totally tapped out, and it gave me a special thrill.

The tips were often the best part of these nights. There was one night when I was doing okay, getting good, steady business, when I got flagged down by a guy on Sixth Avenue and Bleecker Street. There are some restaurants there that people always want cabs from.

This guy leaned in the window and said, "Turn on the meter. We just need to wait for our friends to come out."

Again with the waiting, but I hit the meter anyway and watched as he and his buddy stood there and smoked cigarettes, waiting for their dates to emerge from the restaurant. The minutes started ticking by, marked by a forty-cent click for every two, and by the time the meter reached $4.10—eight precious minutes after I turned it on at $2.50—I was on the verge of leaving.

I rolled down the window and said, "What's up? You guys getting in or what?"

The first guy leaned over and said, "Yeah, here they come now. Thanks for waiting. And, don't worry, we're big tippers."

That was all I needed to hear.

The women wobbled over in their high heels, and the whole group hopped in, with the self-proclaimed big tipper getting in front next to me. They were in a fantastic mood, laughing and joking, and the guy sitting next to me tried to include me in the fun. I, however, was in work mode and couldn't really party along. The guy introduced himself as Chaz and offered me a piece of gum, which led the girls in the back to comment on what great teeth he had.

I tried to be a good sport, to smile and laugh along, but it wasn't easy. I was tired and operating in a totally different reality from them. For me, they were just another fare in a long, tiring series of fares. I was dirty and sweaty and had been sitting for too long already. Meanwhile, they were emerging from a nice expensive dinner and going on their way to a night of high-priced alcohol, hairspray, and cologne, and I was an intermediate character in their night. Which was fine, I guess. Sometimes I'm not even noticed *that* much by my passengers.

They wanted to go to a relatively new and, apparently, hot club called Marquee. "Do you know where it is?" Chaz asked.

"I think so. Is that the one on Twenty-seventh and Tenth?"

"That's the one. How much do you think it'll cost to get there?"

Great, I thought, *now he's worried about the money. Shit.*

"Ummm, probably like eight or nine dollars?"

"Okay, I'm just trying to figure out how much to tip you."

Trying to keep my humor, I replied, "You work on that and get back to me."

He said, "How's five dollars sound?"

I laughed and said, "That's okay, but fifty would be better," hoping he'd catch it as a joke and laugh along.

He did, and continued, "Twenty?"

I decided to keep going up instead of down. "I think a hundred would do."

He also kept going up. "Forty?"

"Two hundred."

Hearing this, the girls in the back got upset and risked ruining their manicures when they started hitting the partition.

"She's trying to take advantage of you, Chaz! That's so messed up!"

Chaz gave me a little wink as he turned around in his seat and closed the partition window, drowning out the girls' voices. Then he waved at them and stuck his tongue out.

When we pulled up in front of the club, the meter read $9.40.

He said, "Uh-oh, you said eight or nine dollars, but now it's nine forty. That wasn't part of our arrangement."

I couldn't tell anymore if he was kidding, so I just didn't say anything. With a look of mischief, Chaz pulled out his wallet, handed me a bill, and said, "Keep it."

I looked down and saw it was a fifty. Holding it up to him in the light, I said, "Are you sure?"

He said, "Yes! I *told* you we were good tippers!"

And with that, they got out. I sat there for a second and watched as they crossed the huge mosh of people outside the velvet ropes, shook the bouncer's hand, and were ushered directly inside, VIP-style.

An hour or two later, as I was cruising down Ninth Avenue, a woman hailed me from a bus stop. When she got in, she said, "I couldn't stand waiting for the bus anymore. It's freezing out!" And then, "I'm sorry, but this will be a short ride."

Each cabbie seems to have a different opinion about whether short rides are better than long rides. For me, it depended on a number of variables such as time of day, traffic, level of business on the streets, and destination. During normal hours when business is good, it ultimately came down to a difference of a few dollars, so it wasn't that big a deal. But if it was late or business was slow, I preferred the longer rides since there was little chance of finding a bunch of short ones that added up to the same amount. Most often, though, the long rides were one-way deals, meaning I'd have to go back to Manhattan empty, so they usually didn't pay off that well anyway.

But the greatest lesson I learned after only my first few months as a cabbie was to just take what you can get and not get too upset about it. This helped me when I'd have to go on long one-ways to Brooklyn or Queens or the Bronx a million times a night, areas where I was guaranteed to not find a fare on my way back to the more cab-friendly Manhattan. There's an inherent lack of choice and control in this job, and I had by then, thankfully, figured out how to not let that part of it get to me.

That night, I was already relaxed and happy with my shift, so I reassured the woman in my backseat who was worried about her short trip. "Don't worry about it. Money's money. Every dollar counts."

We chatted a little about nothing in particular and, roughly three minutes later, pulled up in front of her building. The meter read $3.80. She handed me a twenty and said, "Keep the change. You're doing a great job."

A little while later, three girls got in and we drove up First Avenue. As we passed NYU Medical Center on 31st Street, one of the girls saw the sign and said, "Oh, NYU. This is the area where Becca got her leather jacket and tattoo."

Looking around the residential east side neighborhood, one of the other girls said, "Oh really? It doesn't look *that* cool around here."

I found this highly amusing, especially since we were nowhere near Greenwich Village, where the actual NYU academic buildings were. When they got out, I put my earpiece in and called Allie to tell her about it. I knew if I didn't relay the story to her right away, I would probably forget about it. Allie had a computer-like memory. She was able to recall any story, movie, or even entire sections of books word for word. I, on the other hand, had a memory made of Swiss cheese, so I had taken to storing my own experiences in her brain in case I wanted to retrieve them later on.

When she picked up, I said, "The funniest conversation just

happened and I need you to remember it 'cause I know I'll forget it immediately." I told her about the girls who thought we were near NYU and she got a little kick out of it.

"I also got two amazing tips tonight."

"That's great!" She sounded genuinely happy. She knew I'd been having kind of a hard time lately.

She was quiet for a moment, clearly distracted by something else. "What are you doing?" I asked.

"Trying to write this outline for the show. Did I tell you? They're not letting me write a script. But of course they're letting *Heather* write an episode. I'm so annoyed." Heather was the other junior writer on the TV show Allie was working on. They got hired at the same time, but Heather was dating one of the producers, so she got preferential treatment.

Allie continued, "But, listen, I'm right in the middle of this. I can't really talk right now. Can I call you tomorrow?"

I drove around for a few more hours without incident. It appeared that my good mood was contagious because all my subsequent passengers were extra nice, and most of them even tipped me decently. It was one of the few shifts where I ended the night actually feeling good.

Then there were the nights when everything seemed to go wrong, but all it took was for one good thing to happen to make it all seem okay again. This happened one Thursday night near the beginning of summer when traffic was so apocalyptic I truly thought the world must be ending—that it was the final Last Day and everyone was instinctively fleeing the city. There was no other rational explanation for the hours upon hours upon hours of backups and gridlock and tunnel closures and general fuckedness on the streets that night. And, after a while, I actually *hoped* that the world was coming to an end so that I could be put out of my misery.

I had, by that point, built up a decent threshold of traffic tolerance, but once I crossed it, there was no going back.

I could usually deal with heavy rush-hour traffic for about four, maybe five, hours. But after that, if rush hour didn't go away, my nerves began to fray.

So this night, after the eighth hour of my shift, when I still couldn't move anywhere, I just dropped off my last passenger in Brooklyn and called it a night.

When I got back to the garage, Paul the crazy Romanian dispatcher offered up some choice wisdom. He said, "You need three sets of balls to do this job. I wouldn't wish it on my worst enemy, that's how fucked it is."

Before he became a dispatcher/cashier, Paul put 650,000 miles under his belt as a cabbie. Calling it "the worst job in the world," Paul was always telling me I should be doing something else. And he was right. My nerves were so totally shot, I couldn't even begin to imagine driving in the city for another three or four hours after that to finish out the shift, especially since the traffic was STILL bad. But that was just me. I figured I'd give myself a break. Of course, plenty of other cabbies stayed out and braved it for the full twelve hours, I just didn't have the heart for it.

Paul went into story mode, saying, "My first day as a cab driver—July Fourth, 1990—I wasn't excited. I didn't want to meet new people. Who the hell do you meet in this job? A new kind of asshole, that's who. And those guys making seventy-thousand-plus? They're not setting foot in your yellow car. They have their little car services and the company pays for it. Cab drivers are just sweeping the streets. It's only every now and then you meet a halfway decent human being in the cab, and what is that? Maybe once a shift? Less than that? No way, man. Like I said, I wouldn't wish this job on my worst enemy."

But, in fact, that night I had met one halfway decent human being in my cab. I'd picked him up and proceeded to immediately get stuck in horrendous traffic going up First Avenue at

10:00 P.M. He remarked on it, wondering aloud what the hell was going on.

I just said, "It's been like this all day, but I have no idea why. And it's everywhere." But at that point, the already-bad situation was made even worse because it had rained and the FDR was flooded from the downpour, which meant that every single car in the universe (or so it seemed) was driving up First and Third. Going any farther west would've made no difference because Park had construction blocking two lanes, Madison was already a parking lot, and the entire west side had been clogged up all day and, even at that hour, showed no signs of improving. There was truly no escape.

We stayed on First and inched our way ever so slowly up to his destination at 116th and Lex. Luckily, this guy was totally relaxed and unconcerned about the traffic or the meter or the route or much of anything. Instead, we had pleasant conversation to keep our minds off the mess we were stuck in.

At one point, we got on the topic of video games. "Sometimes, after a night like this, I go home and play Grand Theft Auto and just run everyone over," I said.

He perked up and said, "Which one? San Andreas or Vice City?"

"San Andreas."

He shared a story about a friend of his who was a bike messenger in the city and who, after playing San Andreas for a little too long, started seeing "hidden packages" all around New York, blurring the real streets into video game reality. This was an impulse in which I, unfortunately, could not indulge, since the result would definitely have been bloody and probably would've ended in my arrest.

We traded tips and strategies, and compared notes on the game. At the end of the ride, he wished me luck and gave me a massive tip, nearly 70 percent of the metered fare. And that was all it took—just one nice guy, a pleasant, fun conversation, and an appreciative tip—to keep me afloat for another full hour, even though I'd felt like giving up hours earlier.

When I did finally quit and drive back to Brooklyn in the Buick, I listened as the traffic reporters were still calling the situation in the city a "nightmare." I thought of the cabbies still struggling on the streets to make the night pay off, and felt like I was cheating a little bit by quitting early. But I also felt relief that I didn't have to deal with it anymore. When I got home, instead of playing San Andreas, I just passed out, happily lacking the three sets of required balls.

Of course, there were plenty of nights when luck really turned against me, and nothing could turn it around. Everything seemed to go wrong and snowballed into a giant ball of crap and aggravation. I'd get stuck behind a slow-moving, cell-phone-talking idiot driving his fancy midlife-crisis speedster at five miles per hour, or a wimpy SUV slowing down for every pothole, or a Jersey hooptie exuding pot smoke out its windows. A garbage truck would trap me on a street for twenty or thirty minutes without a passenger. I'd lose fares to other, more aggressive cabbies. All night long, I'd strain at the leash trying to move, but there was nowhere to go. Every obstacle, no matter how big or small, would only add to my stress level, and a few hours into the shift, I'd feel like I was about to have a stroke.

On one of these nights in particular, I knew something was wrong from the very beginning. Something must've been in the air because everyone on the streets was super-aggressive and pissed off and driving like shit. The traffic was satanic and people were noticeably edgy. Early on, a refined young Jersey driver made an illegal right turn on red down Ninth Avenue, where I happened to be driving. When he almost hit me, he flipped out and sped up next to me, and was generous enough to throw me my favorite sign, the ubiquitous and meaningless middle finger. Oh, right, sorry, I guess it was my fault for trying to go through a green light. Then he rolled down his window and told me he was going to kick my ass.

I said, "Be my guest," but he didn't move. He just kept screaming.

Meanwhile, cars were whizzing around us, horns were blaring, and we were stopped in the middle of it all because he blocked me in and refused to move out of the way. Guess he wasn't in such a big hurry after all, since he was clearly more interested in spending his precious time threatening me. When he finally got his fill of this, he peeled out like a real tough guy and sped down the avenue.

The night could only get better from there. Which it did later on when I got hit by a bus.

Actually, it wasn't so much a hit as it was a clip. I was sitting at a red light on Battery Place when the bus in the lane on my left pulled up too close and crunched a glass pane of its door against my driver-side mirror. I sat there and watched in helpless horror, unable to move the car. The mirror got pushed forward and the glass on the bus door shattered.

When I finally pulled up so I could get out and check out the damage, a Metropolitan Transportation Authority (MTA) guy jumped off the bus and started yelling at me. As we were standing there in the middle of traffic, he came over, got in my face, and screamed, "What the fuck is wrong with you? Are you fucking blind?"

I couldn't believe it. I pointed at the cab and said, "Look at my mirror! It's pushed FORWARD. Unless I was driving in reverse, it could not have been my fault!"

As I'd learned early on, taxi mirrors are extremely resilient, and this time I was able to just flip it back into position, but I was pissed that this guy was trying to blame it on me. We were still arguing when another MTA guy came over and said, "I'm the driver of this bus. Is there any damage to your car?"

I checked the cab and said no. Then he said, "Okay, let's just forget about it. This never happened."

We would both have lost our nights if either of us pursued an accident report, so I agreed to just let it go. We shook hands and I got back into the cab.

Back in midtown later, as I was stopped at a light, from out of nowhere, the driver of the cab next to me jumped out and started banging on my window. He was screaming something I couldn't make out because police cars were screaming past us, blowing through the red lights, keeping traffic at a halt, and all I could hear was the blare of their sirens. Then a passenger came up from the other side and was trying to get into the cab, so I chose to not roll my window down and get into it with the other cabbie. I never did figure out what his problem was, but his aggression fit right in with the overall vibe of the night.

To cap off the evening, I got hit again, this time by another cab. I was exiting the Brooklyn-Queens Expressway onto McGuinness Boulevard in Brooklyn when the cab next to me decided to change lanes—despite the fact that I happened to be IN that lane—and he hit me.

When I started to write down his medallion number, he flipped out. We pulled over in front of a gas station and he insisted on calling the cops, even though there was no real damage to either cab. It was such a total waste of time. I was already drained and angry from this whole night of shit, and when he wouldn't stop yelling at me, I snapped and yelled, "Do you have kids? Because bad things are going to happen to them now."

I just wanted him to shut the fuck up already, and it worked. Luckily, I had a really cool passenger, a pretty girl who said she worked in a "massage parlor," which I took to mean she gave hand jobs for a living. She stayed in the cab with me and waited for the police to arrive.

When they finally showed up a half hour later, they filled out an accident report and sent us on our respective ways—but not before the night reached its pinnacle of absurdity when one of the cops made a pass at my passenger, taking out his cell phone and asking for her number. She didn't give it.

By this time, she and I had been on this trip together for forty-five minutes. When we crossed over the Pulaski Bridge into Queens, she told me she was hungry and asked if I could do her a favor and pull through the drive-through at Wendy's so she could pick up some food. She had been so patient and nice about the whole accident/cops thing, I figured it was the least I could do.

After I dropped her off, it was already late. I decided to call it quits and get rid of this bad-luck cab, be done with this weird-ass night. When I pulled into the garage, I was a little nervous about what Paul the crazy Romanian dispatcher was going to say to me. I had called him throughout the night to report each incident, so he knew what had happened, and I felt no small amount of trepidation when I saw him standing at the gas pumps as I rolled in.

I guess he felt sorry for me, though, because when he saw me, he gave a big smile and said, "Look who it is! Welcome back from Iraq!"

Paul being nice was an unexpected gift. I paid my lease for the night and sat down at the table to fill out an accident report for the garage while Paul stood outside the booth smoking a cigarette and telling me stories about accidents he'd gotten into when he was a driver, giving me tips on how to get out of tickets. His thick Romanian accent was a comfort just then.

He said, "So I pull an illegal left turn off Fifty-seventh Street and the cops are there, just waiting for me. I roll down my window and, when the cop comes up, I just say, 'I know. I'm a fucking idiot.' The cop laughed and let me go."

He went on, "If you're not lucky, you gotta be smart, or you won't make any money. Another time, I got pulled over and I said to the cop, 'You're fucking me good now. This was supposed to be my last night as a cab driver. I hate this fucking job. I have an appointment tomorrow to take the bus driver test for the MTA, but now I'll have points on my license and my new career is already over. Don't stick me with driving a cab forever.' The guy felt bad for me and let me go."

I was just relieved that Paul wasn't going nuts on me. I think he sensed that yelling at me wouldn't do either of us any good. It's not like I willed these accidents to happen. Besides, all the garage really cared about was that the cab wasn't damaged, so I guess I was lucky in that regard.

When he wasn't putting me in a headlock or telling me that he was going to leave his wife for me, Paul occasionally revealed his more sensitive side. He would say, "I hate seeing you show up here. This is a dead-end job. You're not like these fucking idiots over here. I want to see you get out of this business." And other times, after I arrived at the garage in the afternoon, he would say, "You made my day. I just got hard seeing your car pull in!"

When he was dispatching me, I also got called a series of names over the loudspeaker. Sometimes I was "Melissa the beautiful," other times "Melissa the cute." After being out sick, he would call me "Melissa the sick fuck." This was tame compared to some of his more creative appellations, my favorites being "Murray Salami," "Jacob the crook," "Igor KGB," "Boris the genius," "Ahmed al-Qaeda," and "Mamadou my gay lover," to name just a few.

I had come to appreciate Paul. There were so many rumors

about him at the garage, I didn't know what to believe. Supposedly he'd been a supporter of Romania's Communist dictator, Ceauşescu, and had fled the country in 1989 after Ceauşescu was overthrown. I didn't know if this was true, nor did I really care.

Regardless of his past, he was an incredibly sharp man with a strange imagination. He was alternately cruel and sweet, and the guys at the garage either loved or hated him. Still, we all knew to expect the unexpected out of him. Occasionally he would push a guy too far and they would quit or complain to David about him, but as long as he gave me a cab when I needed one and didn't abuse me *too* hard or *too* often, I liked him.

It was three in the morning and I was finishing up the accident report when some other night drivers started trickling in, cutting their shifts an hour short. Helen was among them, as was a pompous young Arab American guy named Nicholas. He was about twenty-two years old and I didn't like him.

This guy was always bragging about how much money he made each night, showing off about how much he overcharged his passengers for out-of-town fares, and so on. He was nice enough in general, I suppose, but he was also sort of annoying and immature. This was the guy who, months later, hit a man on a bicycle with his cab and then left the scene. He called Omar, the cashier on duty that night, and said, "I just hit a guy. I'm down the street. Should I go back?" Omar was like, "Yes, go back right away. What the hell were you thinking?" He went back and promptly got arrested. The garage tried to fire him, but he kept showing up every day until finally they decided to give him another chance.

Anyway, Helen was standing at the dispatch window paying her lease fee, when Nicholas started in on a story about how he took a guy to LaGuardia during rush hour. He said, "It was five o'clock and this yuppie white guy wanted to go to the airport. Traffic was so bad and there were no other cabs, so I told him I'd only do it for double the meter. The guy was in such a hurry and desperate for me to take him, so he agreed."

He clearly thought he was clever for overcharging his passenger, and I think he half expected us to be impressed or something, but when Helen heard this, she was the opposite of impressed. She was infuriated. She started yelling at him, saying, "It's fucks like you who hurt this industry. You're ripping off the public and the rest of us get blamed for it."

Nicholas immediately went on an attack of his own, saying to Helen, "Shut the fuck up. What do *you* know? Have you looked at yourself in the mirror lately?"

Upon hearing this last comment, Helen said, "Great. Another fucking homophobe. You know, most people who say that kind of thing only know what they're talking about because they recognize it in themselves."

The whole time this was happening, Paul remained uncharacteristically silent. The fighting and cursing continued, until finally I started pulling Helen out the door. "Come on," I said. "Let's just go. I'll give you a ride to the subway."

As we walked past him on our way out, Nicholas screamed, "Fucking faggot!"

Helen just said, "Fuck you," and we walked to my car.

I said, "Just forget about him, everyone knows he's an asshole."

"I know, I know. But I can't stand it when I see idiots like him hurt the business and give us the bad reputation that makes the public hate cab drivers so much. *And* he's a fucking homophobe, to boot!"

When we got buckled into the Buick and pulled out of the garage, Helen turned to me and said, "And how was *your* night, my dear?"

CHAPTER 15

Summer in New York is relatively empty. The college students are gone, the well-off customers have retreated for the whole season to their houses upstate or in the Hamptons, and the middle-class citizens work through the week and then every weekend flee the oppressive humidity to Fire Island, the Jersey shore, or Connecticut. Business slows down tremendously and competition between cabbies gets brutal.

Every shift throughout the summer, everywhere I turned, there were more and more empty cabs, spreading and multiplying like an evil virus. The most basic strategy of the job is to be the first empty cab on the block. If there's another empty cab nearby, work the side of the street that he's not on. If you're behind one or more of these guys, slow down so that you're at least two blocks behind them, or turn onto a different street.

But when it's slow, there are just too many to compete with. You could spend hours without a single fare. And it doesn't even matter anymore if you're the first cab in one of the side lanes. If there's a person with their arm up on the next block, you can count on having to race with the cab speeding up from the middle lane, trying to beat you to them.

What makes this situation even worse is that most passengers don't realize what's happening and don't think too much about the fairness of the situation. They just get into the cab that reaches them first, even if it's the one that just cut you off and nearly caused an accident. And then these people have not only gotten into a cab with a desperate animal driving, but they have just helped to create another, even more desperate, and now very angry, animal driving the cab behind them.

There are several ways we try to punish one another for this type of behavior. Sometimes the cut-off cab will stop in front of the guy who just poached his fare and put it into park, making it impossible for him to move without putting it into reverse. Sometimes we'll pull right up to the guy and yell something, or just stare meanly. I prefer to take pictures, to capture the asshole's face and medallion number for all time, hoping he will worry that I am from the *New York Post* or the TLC or something.

Rodrigo's strategy was to block the guy in and get out of the cab to yell. He was a big guy and, despite his essential teddy-bear nature, he could be very intimidating. He also happened to know how to curse people out in Hindi. He taught me how to say "fuck you" in this language, and laughed when he described how upset it made the Indian drivers when he'd say this to them. I dutifully memorized the phrase but never used it. I didn't want to get killed *that* badly.

On one of these slow summer nights, my front passenger-side window got stuck in the down position. It refused to go back up, which meant I wouldn't be able to leave the cab if I wanted to stop to eat or go to the bathroom.

My passenger at the time, a guy visiting on business from Boston, tried to help me fix it, but he kept pushing it down, only making it worse. My next passenger happened to be an engineer from Switzerland. He heard me on the phone reporting the problem to Omar at the garage and he jumped into the front at a red light and proceeded to try to fix it as well.

When nothing he tried worked, he said, "If I could take the door off, I could fix it in two seconds." He then explained precisely how. He ended his description of the problem and how to fix it by saying, "But I have to attend a dinner now. I'm sorry." Still, it was kind of him to even offer.

My subsequent passengers, noting the problem, asked, "So what do you do when it rains?" I simply answered, "Luckily it's not raining tonight."

Of course, an hour later, it started to rain.

Thankfully, it wasn't a heavy downpour or anything and it didn't last very long. I kept my backpack and street atlas close to me on the driver's side so they didn't get wet. Three hours later, at around 11:30, I tried the up button again and the window mysteriously decided to respond to it. I did not open it again for the rest of the night, despite the heat.

Another night, the big nonevent of the shift was that I saw another female cab driver. Considering women make up less than 1 percent of the cab-driving population, it was always nice to run into one of these comrades on the streets.

I pulled up to a light and saw a young black lady in a turtle-neck shirt sitting behind the wheel of the cab next to me. I tapped my horn to get her attention and, when she spotted me, she smiled and rolled down her window. I nodded at the cab and asked, "How long you been doing it?"

"Three years."

"Do you like it?"

She answered, "I love it. What about you?"

I said, "Almost a year. And I hate it."

I was really starting to, by then.

She gave me a sympathetic smile as the light changed and we drove away.

Summer crawled by like a slug, and in terms of the job, I couldn't wait for it to be over. Each shift was hard and slow and hot.

August came, and by the end of it, Hurricane Katrina had devastated the Gulf Coast. Gas prices rose astronomically and it got even harder to make the money necessary to make ends meet while having to pay upward of $40 each shift for gas.

I turned thirty on September first and celebrated having been on the job for a full year. For most people, turning thirty can be difficult to accept, but I wasn't too fazed by it. I had been preparing myself for it the entire year. Ever since the moment I turned twenty-nine, if someone asked me how old I was, I would answer, "Almost thirty." So when the big day actually came, it wasn't that big a deal. However, despite my efforts, for the next few months, I would occasionally be stopped in my tracks by the thought, *I'm thirty years old. I live alone with two cats. And I'm a cab driver.*

As my luck would have it, I ended up getting food poisoning from my birthday dinner at a fancy restaurant in Brooklyn and was out of commission for the next three days.

Two weeks later, the United Nations General Assembly convened, and I experienced one of the most difficult traffic situations yet. It seemed like the job was only getting harder with each shift. Gas prices kept rising, traffic was increasing, business was slowing, and my energy and will to keep going were flagging.

Driving in New York is a test of one's nerves even on a typical weekday, but when you add the presence of the president and a bunch of foreign dignitaries, the city transforms into one giant parking lot. Cars were not allowed to drive anywhere near the U.N., so First Avenue and the FDR anywhere near midtown were off-limits, which forced everyone to stuff themselves into the clogged drain known as Third Avenue. To make matters even worse, the president was staying at the Waldorf-Astoria, as he always did, so parts of Park and Lexington also became no-drive zones. And whenever the president or his wife moved from event to event, the cops would "freeze" traffic, which meant no one moved an inch for at least twenty minutes. Even the side streets were closed all across the east side, and lanes were blocked off up and down the avenues and major crosstown thoroughfares, like 42nd and 57th Streets, for "emergency traffic." The only real alternative would have been to head to the west side, except that year, Fashion Week was being held at the same time in Bryant Park, on Sixth Avenue behind the main branch of the New York Public Library, which caused a world of hellish traffic on its own. So the west side provided zero relief. Simply put, it was gridlock city.

As was to be expected, the first third of my shift was pure crap. At one point early on, I tried to let a passenger out on the left side of Second Avenue at 43rd Street, when a cop walked over and slammed the lady's door shut in her face. He then screamed at me to drop off on the other side of the avenue. Meanwhile, a police cruiser put his lights on behind me so I would move out of his more-important-than-me way, but the traffic was so heavy, I had to wait for all the cars behind me to get a red light in order to safely move over. It was stressful, to say the least.

Luckily, most of my passengers were understanding, telling me to drop them off as close to their destinations as possible and offering to walk the remaining blocks since they realized that would probably be quicker anyway.

Really, all my rush-hour passengers were cool, except one. It was 5:30 when a woman jumped in at 18th and Third. "Where to?" Her answer: "Fifty-seventh and Fifth." The middle of the hornet's nest, rush hour's ground zero. It was the middle of midtown, and it was not my favorite intersection to begin with. During a normal weekday rush hour, this area was nothing less than a clogged artery, packed with a thousand charter buses and slow-moving cars and frustrated cops, where even wailing ambulances couldn't move because there was never any room for the cars around them to get out of the way. It was enough to give even the most Zen drivers a coronary, so with all the traffic madness happening in the city that day, I didn't want to go anywhere near it.

I turned to the woman and said, "Okay, but I have to warn you, it's going to take a really long time. Are you sure you don't want to just take the subway? I can take you to the closest station."

She was a young Indian-looking woman with an English accent, seemingly very rich and sophisticated. She replied, "No. You have no choice. You have to take me where I want to go. Now move."

Okay, bitch. I already knew where this was heading and I desperately wanted to just kick her out of my cab right then and there, but she was right: I had no real choice. It was illegal to refuse a fare unless they were drunk or disorderly. I could get in trouble for it, and she seemed like just the type of self-righteous asshole that would actually call 311 and file a complaint.

I tried Madison first. It was completely stopped all the way down to its beginning at 23rd Street. Then Sixth Avenue, which was just as bad, with Fashion Week screwing everything up over there. Eighth Avenue was the same, but I figured it was my best bet at that point. When the woman suggested I try 10th Avenue, I explained to her that all the cars, trucks, and buses trying to enter the Lincoln Tunnel would be going that way. Staying true to her stupid bossy nature, she insisted I try it anyway.

Of course, I was right—10th Avenue was a virtual parking lot. After twenty minutes of sitting on the same block, I finally got close enough to the intersection to turn off and get back to Eighth. The whole time this was happening, the woman was having a screaming fight with someone on her cell phone, which only added to the stress.

Finally, an hour after I picked her up, during which we traveled 3.34 miles, we reached 57th and Seventh, two blocks from her destination. I watched the same traffic light change no less than five times until I looked at her and said, "Lady, are you sure you don't want to walk from here? It's just two blocks, and at this rate, we're not gonna get there for at least another twenty minutes."

The meter was at $18.70. She crumpled up a $20 bill and threw it at me, saying meanly, "You really shouldn't be doing this job."

After she got out, I decided against running her over in the intersection when I finally got off 57th and turned south down Seventh Avenue.

Luckily, the rest of my passengers that night were really understanding about the traffic, and that helped me get through the shift. One guy even tried to recruit me to the Landmark Forum, telling me I could "be more effective in life if I put the past in the past in order to create the future," or some shit like that. He himself contributed to my future by tipping a generous eighty cents.

■　　　■　　　■

Three weeks before Halloween, I ended up in Williamsburg around midnight. I had been having pretty good luck during the shift and was taking a passenger to Bedford Avenue and South First Street when, as we were passing South Third, some young thug walked out into the middle of the street without even looking.

When I screeched to a stop in order to avoid hitting him, all his hoodlum buddies on the sidewalk started screaming, "Learn how to drive, bitch!" and other such niceties. It was irritating, but I kept driving while my drunk female passenger rambled about how poorly these idiots treat women and so on until finally, two blocks later, she remembered she needed to pay me and get out.

After that I got a fare to South 11th and Berry, still in Williamsburg. When I was dropping the guy off, there was a cop car blocking the street, facing the wrong way, and the cops were writing a ticket to an illegally parked truck. Clearly this was important business they needed to take care of at 12:30 in the morning, and they apparently didn't like that I was using the street as, you know, a roadway. I had to drop the guy off in front of them because I couldn't get past them. They apparently didn't like that either and they buzzed their little siren thing at me a couple of times while I pulled over.

They finished writing up the ticket, stuffed it into the door of the truck, and finally moved out of my way. As they passed me, they gave dirty, smirky looks, and I, in turn, gave them a wide, obnoxious smile, as I realized the finger was probably not the smartest option there.

I decided to cruise back up Bedford since the city was already dead when I left it. As I passed South Third again, the thugs were still there and they recognized me. I heard them say, "That's the same bitch from before!" And the next second there was a loud, violent crack next to my head. I felt a viscous wetness on my hair and my arm, and when I reached up to touch it, I half expected to see blood on my fingertips. However, I quickly realized that my driver-side window—which was halfway down—the inside of my windshield, and my left arm were covered not with blood but with egg yolk.

After realizing what had just happened, I stopped the car and considered. I was pissed and my first and most tempting instinct was to back up and mow the thugs down with my cab, but that seemed a bit extreme.

My second instinct was to take out my phone and pretend to call the cops (pretend, since I didn't think they would've appreciated a 911 call for egg on my window), which I did, but then I felt sort of ridiculous.

Finally, I decided to just find a cop on the street somewhere. Of course now, when I wanted them, there were no cops to be found. When I spotted a cruiser ten minutes later, I told them what had happened and followed them back to my little crime scene.

The thugs were gone. The cops turned left down South Third, going the wrong way on the one-way street, and I wasn't sure if I should follow them, so I just continued straight up Bedford. Maybe I should've gone with them, but by that time I was so tired and defeated I just went off-duty and drove back to the garage.

When I got there and told the guys what had happened, one of my fellow drivers was mildly shocked, exclaiming, "But it's not even Halloween yet!"

I could feel myself becoming hardened, and it was not long after that when I did my first purposefully dishonest act. I was in Chelsea when I picked up a tall, young, lanky hipster guy with black hair. It was on the late side of another slow night and he wanted to go to Williamsburg. I was glad to have the job.

He directed me to the nice, gentrified, expensive part of the neighborhood where the thugs didn't hang out anymore. When we stopped in front of his newly renovated warehouse-loft conversion building, the meter was at \$15. He handed me a bill and said, "Just give me four back."

I thought, *Great, another shitty tip from an overprivileged hipster.* A \$1 tip on a \$15 fare is not appropriate. It's not even *10* percent, much less the 15 or 20 that would be fitting.

I was a little offended, but then, for just a fraction of a second, I looked at the bill. It was a fifty. I was pretty sure he thought it was a twenty, so I confirmed, saying, "*Four* back?"

In a huffy, clipped tone, he said, "Yes," like he was in a big hurry and I was slowing him down.

The weird part of it was that at the garage that afternoon, I'd had a conversation about just this type of thing. When Daniel came in, he told a story about how he felt bad because he'd accidentally accepted a fifty the night before. His passengers thought it was a twenty but he only realized it later when he was counting up his money.

A few other drivers, two knuckleheads named Murray and Sid, were hanging around, and upon hearing this, they said, "Who cares? Think about all the people who stiffed you on the tip. You deserve that money!"

I joined the conversation and said, "No way, man. I don't think I could live with myself if I did that. Just this week I had two people accidentally give me twenties they thought were tens. When I realized their mistake, I corrected them. And they always appreciated it."

Murray asked, "Did they give you a bigger tip?"

"No, but that's not the point. The point is it's dishonest."

Then Sid said, "Screw honesty, it's all about the benjamins. I always take what they give me, no questions asked. If it's a mistake, it's *their* problem, not mine."

I didn't agree. We've all been on the other end of a money mistake and we all know how good it feels when the person who could benefit from it is honest and gives it back. Besides, people need to trust their cab drivers if they're going to take cabs. They need to know they're not gonna get raped or robbed or ripped off. Otherwise the industry would die and none of us would make *any* money.

But for whatever reason, that night—maybe because business was slow, or maybe because I was insulted by his intended shitty tip, or maybe because I judged him for living in the nice part of Williamsburg—instead of correcting the hipster's mistake, I just said, "All right."

I put the fifty on the seat next to me and tried to pretend to myself that I hadn't noticed it. There wasn't really time to think about what I was doing, I just did it. I counted out four singles, handed them to him through the partition, and he got out.

I imagined him realizing his mistake later and thinking what an asshole I was. I thought about him never tipping a cab driver again, or filing the experience in along with everyone else's shitty cab driver stories. I felt guilty.

Looking for comfort, I called Helen.

"Guess what just happened?"

"What? You got a ride to Jersey?"

"No. I took a fifty that the guy thought was a twenty—and I didn't say anything."

"Oh. We were just talking about that this afternoon."

"I know. I don't feel very good about it."

"Do you have a pit in your stomach?"

"Yeah."

"Well, it'll go away eventually, but it's not a nice feeling."

"No, it isn't."

I felt jinxed after that, like it was inevitable that some bad karma was going to come my way in the form of an accident or a ticket or a fare-beater, so I hit my off-duty light and just headed back to the garage. The whole way back I promised myself I would never do that again, no matter how big the asshole was in the back of the cab. It just wasn't who I wanted to be.

I decided things were gonna be different from that moment on. Cabbies already had a reputation for being heartless money-hungry rip-off artists, and I didn't want to feed into that. There were already enough drivers who satisfied this stereotype, but there were also plenty more who were good, decent human beings. They were the ones who committed small, and sometimes entirely unnoticed, acts of kindness for strangers, acts that were not financially motivated, or sometimes acts that even *cost* them money. It was usually not a huge, life-changing gesture, but still, it counted for something. Sometimes it simply consisted of returning a found phone, or turning in lost luggage, or giving a free ride to someone who really needed it. Or, like one cabbie whose story actually made it into the news, returning thousands of dollars worth of jewels that were left in a suitcase in the trunk. There was another famous story about a guy who returned a valuable violin. But I knew there were countless other small acts that no one outside the industry ever heard about.

One of my small acts of kindness came a few weeks later and it took the form of waiting. It was late and I picked up a young black woman going to the Bronx, 165th Street and Washington, to be precise. I wasn't thrilled about going up there, but I got on the FDR and made it in pretty good time. The meter at the end of the trip read $22.80 and I received a handsome twenty-cent tip. With only two exceptions, I was never tipped for a job to the Bronx, so this was no big surprise.

But when it was time for the girl to get out of the cab, she looked over and saw a strange man lingering on her stoop. It was around 4:00 A.M. and there was no one else on the street— just me and her in the cab, and this man in front of her building. She leaned up to the partition and said, "I'm afraid to get out with that man standing there. Do you mind waiting here with me until my boyfriend shows up? He's on his way already."

I said, "Maybe he lives in the building and got locked out? Do you recognize him?"

She replied, "He's probably waiting to be let in, but I don't know him. He definitely doesn't live in my building. And he looks damn shady, don't he?"

I agreed, and knowing I couldn't live with myself if I let her get out of the cab like that, I told her I'd wait. She got on the phone to her boyfriend to hurry him up.

"Where are you? . . . Oh, okay. Well, hurry up. There's some man standing in front of the building hanging out. . . . No, I'm still in the cab. . . . The driver's a lady, she's staying with me. . . . Okay, bye."

I wanted a cigarette badly by that point, but I didn't have a light. I asked the girl if she had a match and she said, "Yeah, you can have these," handing me a book of them. Then, "Can I smoke too?"

Figuring it was my last job of the night, I said yes, and we each lit up and cracked the windows. We sat there and smoked in silence.

After a few minutes, my phone rang with Rodrigo on the other end.

"Yo, what's up? I'm at the garage, but Omar said you didn't get back yet. I thought you were coming in."

"Yeah, I'm in the Bronx. My passenger can't get out because some scary guy is standing on her stoop. I'll be back soon."

"Oh, okay. I was a little worried."

"No, I'm fine. I have all the doors locked just in case."

"Okay, see you in a few."

I hung up and finished my cigarette. I thought for a second about how I was going to be late back to the garage and all I had gotten from this girl was a twenty-cent tip. In the past, I might not have been so generous, but I had learned a thing or two from Daniel, who always went out of his way for people, and he seemed a happier man because of it. And I had realized by then that sometimes money is the least important part of the job. Sometimes it was worth losing a few bucks, or a few minutes, in order to do some actual good in the world. I knew I was doing the right thing, and that was all that mattered.

Just as the boyfriend called to say he was almost there, we saw another man walk out of the building and shake hands with the shady guy on the stoop. They both looked around and starting walking up the street, away from the building. Finally, when they were gone, the girl decided it was safe to go. She thanked me for waiting and got out of the cab. I sat for another few seconds to make sure she got inside okay, and then I turned around and got the hell out of there.

CHAPTER 16

People are strong, and yet so fragile, too. I'm always amazed at how easily we are hurt, how our skin can be cut by mere paper on the one hand, and how our bodies can be smashed to pieces by oncoming cars, on the other. How we can be eaten away from the inside by an invisible disease or have our hearts broken by harsh words.

But even more amazing is how we survive these things, how we get up and brush ourselves off and move on. When I was hit by a car, I tried to get up but couldn't. I fell back to the ground in the middle of the street and watched the Friday afternoon traffic swing around me up and down the street until I was scooped up and carried to the sidewalk by a few sympathetic strangers.

Someone called an ambulance and I was taken to the emergency room at Saint Vincent's hospital. When the EMTs asked me my name and address, I was able to provide the information. But when they asked me what year and month it was, panic set in. I couldn't remember. It took me a while. I had to think about what season it was, what the weather was like outside the ambulance, until finally I came to it—June 2003. Friday the thirteenth, to be exact.

It was 11:30 in the morning and I was on my way to the dentist, crossing the street, when a young guy hit me with the side of his car. It took a while for me to accept that it had really even happened, it just seemed so absurd to get hit by a car.

My foot was broken and my body was bruised and sore, but I had been hit by a two-thousand-pound vehicle and I had *lived*. When I got off the crutches two months later, I learned how to walk using both feet again. My body will probably never be the same, but it adjusted and my life continues almost as if this event never even occurred.

Six months later, long before I ever sat behind the wheel of a yellow cab, I had a fight with a cab driver, and he dragged me down the street while I hung outside the passenger window of the car. It was a small thing at first. A Friday night and three of us were on our way home from the Hole, as usual, making two stops in Brooklyn. When the first person got out, the cabbie turned the meter off and then back on. I turned to my friend and said, "That's bullshit. He just reset the meter."

Upon hearing this, the cabbie started cursing and yelling at me. Words and insults were exchanged until finally I said, "Fuck this, we're getting out." We left the cab but we hadn't paid him. He followed us, screaming out his open passenger-side window that we had better pay him, that he was gonna call the cops, that we were stupid bitches who could suck his dick, and so on.

I decided we better pay him so he would leave us alone and we could go home. I walked up to the passenger-side window and began counting out the exact change. I said, "I want a receipt."

He said, "You'll get it, just give me the money."

When I handed it to him, still leaning halfway in the window, he hit the gas. I was taken by surprise, didn't know what to do. I was being dragged down the street but I held on to the inside of the car, figuring he would slow down so I could walk away without getting hurt.

Instead, he sped up. I stared at him in disbelief but was too shocked to say or do anything, until finally I realized he had no plans to slow down. I let go and tumbled to the street as he flew off. My friend ran up to me and asked if I was okay as I lay on the street for a few minutes, trying to get my head back together enough to figure out what had just happened. I said I was fine and got up. My jeans were ripped in the knee, under which there was a cut, and I had a bump on my head, but other than that, I really was fine. Limping and a little dizzy, we called a car service to take us the rest of the way home. I was nauseous and sore for the next few days but I was back to normal within the week.

I had been lucky. But it seemed like too many people in New York put their luck to the test when it came to man versus car. A common sight from the driver's seat of a cab is of pedestrians crossing the street against the light, usually in the middle of the avenue, where they're even less anticipated. Often they've got big balls, treating their crossing as an act of courage, as their ultimate right, but really it's utter stupidity. So many times I've had to hit the brakes—and the horn—only to have some macho jaywalker give me the finger, as if I was doing something aggressive to them just by driving on the street where they felt like crossing. Guys have punched my hood and made threats, acting all tough, but I knew they wouldn't be so tough with their heads bleeding out under the wheels of my cab. And sometimes it seemed like these people were cutting it so close that they were practically *daring* me to hit them.

The sad thing is, people get knocked down by cars so often in New York, it's almost routine. It's like a bowling alley but without the special shoes. Luckily most cars are rolling slowly enough that their strikes aren't fatal. But that's not always the case.

I had picked up an extra shift on a Tuesday night to make up for a day I had taken off the previous week. I didn't like Tuesdays, always had bad luck on them, but I hoped for the best. It was a mistake.

Business looked good, but I wasn't getting any of it. Everywhere I went was the wrong place to be. There was always another empty cab right in front of me, no matter where I turned, even though most of the other cabs on the street were occupied. I spent a prime hour, between seven and eight, without one single passenger. The stress was getting to me and I was starting to really regret picking up this miserable extra shift.

Finally, I saw a girl with her arm up on Third Avenue and 20th Street, heading uptown. She wanted to go to Third and 48th—not the longest trip. Fine. It's not like I was in any position to be picky.

When we reached 40th Street, cars were backed up everywhere. The avenue was jammed and no one was moving. I saw flashing lights up ahead but thought nothing of it. It was not an unusual sight.

Then emergency vehicles came speeding along from all directions, saturating the area with strobing red and white. An ambulance was heading up Third Avenue behind me, trying to inch through the unmoving cars. The cars squeezed over to let it through until finally it was nosing the trunk of my cab. But I couldn't move until the car in front of me moved. Which it didn't immediately do. I don't know what it was waiting for—did the driver not realize there was an ambulance behind us? The lights were flashing, the sirens were screaming, and the noise was deafening.

The car in front of me still wouldn't budge so I started honking, not making the situation any better, but there was nothing else I could do. I was using my horn to tell the car in front of me to *MOVE,* and, finally, it did.

I got out of the way, leaving just enough room for the ambulance to press past, and then sat for another few minutes waiting for the rest of the cars to inch forward.

At 42nd Street, cops were directing traffic to the left and right, not letting anyone continue north on Third Avenue. It was another five long minutes before I was able to make the turn, heading east. My passenger said, "Just drop me off here, I'll walk the rest of the way." I pulled to the curb and let her out. *Great,* I thought, *now I can't even finish this one goddamn trip.*

I counted out her change and she got out. Sitting there on the corner for a minute feeling miserable, I watched the chaos. I looked behind me at the now-closed Third Avenue and saw a bus stopped in the middle of the intersection. I assumed it had broken down and was the source of all the traffic, until I realized there was a crowd of bystanders staring at the scene.

I rolled down my window and asked two men standing nearby what had happened. They pointed at the bus and said, "Look at the back wheels. There's a guy trapped underneath 'em."

I wish now that I had just driven away, that I hadn't turned around and followed their gaze, that I'd never seen what I saw.

But I did turn. And there, under the giant back wheels of the bus, between the frantic blur of emergency workers and EMTs, I saw the lifeless body of a man. The bus riders had been evacuated and were on the sidewalks, gawking at the horrific scene. More emergency vehicles—cops and fire trucks and ambulances—were arriving, and the cops were closing off the area with police tape, trying to manage the situation, directing traffic and unloading all sorts of equipment.

I froze there, staring at what was left of this man. Through the chaos I glimpsed legs, blood, and other stuff that I couldn't identify. And though it wasn't all perfectly clear, it was something I'd never wanted to see in my life. It was the first few moments of someone's death. That the guy was no longer alive was probably the only thing left in his favor. Unlike so many other downed pedestrians, this guy would not be getting up, brushing himself off, and walking away.

I was frozen there, staring, unable to take it all in and digest the information. I felt something shift and crumble in my chest, like precariously stacked children's blocks crashing down to my stomach. In some jobs, people see death all the time. But my job was to drive, to navigate the city, to sit safely sheltered in a yellow Ford Crown Victoria, a partition separating me from the passengers, a windshield separating me from the world. But here I was, on an already crappy extra shift, witnessing a tragedy. I thought I was tough enough by then to deal with real shit like this, but I guess I wasn't. Not yet, at least.

I finally peeled my eyes away from the scene and looked around. The lights were suddenly too bright, the sounds too loud. The city became a harsh painful place filled with raw skin, blood, and bones. Hostile cops continued screaming at stupid motorists, ambulances kept blaring across 42nd Street and getting trapped in the now-impenetrable gridlock behind me.

I waited for an opening in the cars and pulled back into the traffic. Halfway down the block, I started sobbing. I hit my off-duty light, locked my doors, and let it all out. I turned down Second Avenue and pulled over again. Leaning my head forward on the steering wheel, I whispered out loud to myself, "I can't do this anymore. I can't do this anymore. I can't do this anymore."

I was mad at myself for crying, told myself I was overreacting, being too sensitive, acting like a baby. I mean, it wasn't like *I* was the one who just got hit by a bus. But it all felt so immediate, so dark and haunting and scary. It felt like the city was closing in on me. And, at that moment, I hated my job more than anything in the world.

After sitting there for ten minutes, I realized I was near the café where the girl I'd been dating worked. Her name was Sally and we had started going out a month before, and though I was embarrassed and not sure I wanted her to see me in this condition, I needed to see a friendly face, to be comforted, to have someone treat me with familiarity and tenderness. I parked outside, tried to erase any trace of my crying spell, and went in. Sally was sweet, gave me ice water, and came outside with me to share a cigarette. After a little while, I calmed down and pulled myself together.

I probably should've just quit, cut my shift short and gone home, but something was stopping me. Instead, I got back into the cab and drove around some more, picking up passengers here and there, and waited for Sally to get off work. When she did, I met up with her and a bunch of friends outside a bar in the East Village. A group of us hung out, sitting on the hood of my cab parked on Avenue A, and I tried to forget about the accident. After a while I grew tired and restless and told Sally I was going home. She kissed me goodbye and went inside the bar with her friends.

I intended to call it a night and bring the cab straight back to the garage. At least that was what I *meant* to do. But I guess I wasn't done yet. I still needed something else to *happen,* still needed to process the night somehow, or maybe I just needed a drink. There was a cute girl hanging outside the bar, standing with a friend of mine. They were debating whether or not they should stay there or go have a drink in Williamsburg. I told them I was heading back to the garage through Brooklyn, and if they needed a ride, I would take them where they wanted to go. I wish I could say my intentions were perfectly innocent, but they weren't.

They got into the cab and I drove them to a bar in Brooklyn. They invited me in for a drink but I told them I couldn't, at least not while I still had the cab. "Well, go drop it off and come back. Hang out with us!" said my friend.

When I got back a half hour later, the cute girl bought me a drink and we all sat down. But after five minutes, my friend left, claiming tiredness. I was still a little freaked out by my night, feeling raw and open, and I let the new girl talk at me while handsome young gay boys did karaoke in the background.

At one point she looked at me and said, "This is a good song to make out to."

I leaned in and kissed her. We left shortly afterward and, despite the fact that Sally and I had been getting more serious with each other, I just sort of "accidentally" took this strange girl home with me. At least that's what I told Sally the next day when she called to check on me.

There was really no excuse for it, as Sally never failed to remind me, all the way up until the day we broke up, but I suspect it was a way for me to medicate myself, a way to deal with my shit.

It seemed so easy for my spirit to break just by the sight of one bloody accident, leading me to do something sort of sleazy and out of character, crashing and ultimately destroying what could've been a perfectly good relationship with Sally. The whole year, all the stress and the fights, the tickets and the close calls, the fender benders and the bad dreams, they all came to a sharp point and were distilled into that one stupid

Tuesday night. The city was too big for me. I felt helpless and tiny.

I wanted real life to go away and leave me the hell alone for a minute. I wanted to be someone else for the night, to play a pretend game and act out an alternate version of myself for a few hours with someone who didn't know me, but it was no help. The city was eating away at me like rats chewing on my flesh. It became a part of me that I couldn't shake loose, and it wasn't prepared to let me go without inflicting some small injury.

A few days later at the garage, I told Helen and Rodrigo and Daniel about the accident, but they didn't seem to think much of it. They all said, "Oh, that sucks." I kinda wanted more sympathy.

Instead, Helen told me she had passed by that intersection around three in the morning that night and it was still closed for the investigation the cops have to do when someone dies in an accident. But that was the extent of their reactions. It really wasn't that big a deal in the scheme of things. It was just a part of the job. Certainly, Helen and Daniel had seen far worse things in their years driving. But for me it was a first, a breaking point. I tried to play it off and make light of it, tried not to reveal how seriously I was taking myself, and I joked that there must be a hex on me on Tuesdays. They seemed to buy that I was kidding, but I wasn't. With only one exception that came months later, I refused to work on Tuesdays ever again.

CHAPTER 17

Allie's bicoastal lifestyle finally brought her back to New York for a while. The writing season for the TV show she was working on ended, so she moved back in with her sister in Brooklyn. When I picked her up from Kennedy airport, she was tan and healthy-looking and wore expensive new jeans, but she was still the same old scrounge. She had been so busy in L.A., we hadn't really been talking too much on the phone. While she was there, she didn't have a lot of time for me and our hours were so different, it seemed like she was farther away than she really was. I didn't realize how much I'd missed her until I saw her.

When she got settled in the front seat of my Buick, she spent a few minutes detailing exactly how her left hip felt out of joint. I listened for a while, humoring her through her usual hypochondria, until she got it out of her system and turned her attention to me. "So, what's going on? How's the cab?"

I wanted to act cool, to say something vague and mysterious, to pretend like everything was okay, but this was Allie, my best friend, and I couldn't stop myself from vomiting up my emotional guts.

I took a deep breath and then erupted. "I'm totally fucking miserable. I hate it. And I feel like a goddamn weakling but I just wanna quit. And I can't even do *that,* because in my stupid head I keep hearing a stupid voice that tells me I'm not done yet even though I feel completely beat up and depleted."

Allie listened without interrupting. She knew me well enough to know I just needed to get it out, and that I probably hadn't told anyone else this stuff. She understood me like no one else.

After a few minutes, I ran out of steam and stopped talking. We were taking the back way home, avoiding the highway, and as I turned the car out of the airport, off the JFK Expressway and onto the North Conduit, Allie said, "So when *do* you think it will be enough?"

"I don't know."

I truly didn't. I also didn't know how it could possibly get any better. When I started driving the cab, I was so excited about it, but the novelty had worn off and all my romantic ideas of the job had disappeared. Now it just felt like a job, not an adventure.

Again I was faced with the burden of trying to figure out what to do next. When Allie asked me if I had anything in mind for that, I said, "I don't know. Um, maybe the Peace Corps?"

Allie laughed. "The Peace Corps! You've been talking about that for years!"

I had to stop talking for a second as a speeding car that had been weaving in and out of traffic on the Conduit narrowly cut me off. We were nearing Atlantic Avenue and heading into East New York. We were already almost halfway home.

It was true, I *had* been talking about that for years. Much like I had talked about driving a cab for years before I actually went ahead and did it. The Peace Corps just seemed so much more complicated since I would have to leave the country for two years. But the desire was still there to do something actually *good* in the world. I just wasn't ready yet.

I merged onto Atlantic Avenue finally, then said, "There's also the animal cop thing. You know, like on Animal Planet. I've looked into it, though, and you need two years of law enforcement experience."

Allie said, "What does that even mean, 'two years of law enforcement experience'?"

"I have no idea, but there's no way I'm gonna go and be some shitty cop for two years just because I want to help save the animals. . . . Or maybe I should. I don't fucking know."

We finally made it to Bushwick Avenue. From there it was a straight shot home.

Allie's voice went into her down-to-business mode. "So what can you do now? When we get home, we should make a list and try to figure out what your next step is going to be."

I turned left onto Metropolitan Avenue. The ride was going much more smoothly than I had anticipated. Much better than if I had taken the highway route, which would've been quicker if only there wasn't *always* traffic on the Van Wyck. Better to take an indirect route, skip the traffic, and not get stuck. That was my opinion.

Clearly I wasn't a regular driver anymore. Even in my Buick, in no big rush to get anywhere or to make money, I drove fast and efficiently, constantly trying to figure out the next best move, making sure I avoided a jam. I had developed a certain skill, and now I not only *knew* the back routes and shortcuts, but I *preferred* them half the time. I also knew when to take them and when not to. But I wasn't really thinking about all this right then. I was just bringing my friend home from the airport and trying to figure out what to do with my life. Again.

I thought about Stewie and Daniel and Helen, who had been doing the same job for ten, twenty, thirty years. And, of course, Ricky, who'd been doing it for about ever, but I guess he wasn't such a good example. Somehow, they dealt with it. Sure, they were all completely crazy in their own ways, but they never seemed too traumatized by anything that happened on the job. Everything rolled off their backs. I just couldn't seem to figure out how to do that.

To quit then, no matter how much I was starting to hate it, would've been the biggest ego killer in the world, letting the job defeat me like that. I needed to rise to the challenge somehow, to remember the feeling I had when I first got into it, to see it as an adventure again. I needed to lighten the hell up.

As we pulled up in front of Allie's sister's house, I finally asked about her job and life. Her answer couldn't have been more different from mine.

"So, how's the show? Tell me everything."

"Melissa?" she began, not as a question but rather as a dramatic beat, a preparation for the next sentence, "I couldn't be happier. I've learned more in the past few months than I did in four years of college. It's amazing."

I was happy for her. She really did deserve everything that was happening for her. And I tried very hard to not feel jealous of it as Allie described her perfect new life in sunshiny L.A. as I parked my piece of shit Buick in front of her sister's house.

■   ■   ■

It was Wednesday, "dyke night" at Metropolitan, so Allie and I headed over there to get a few drinks. All the usual girls were in attendance, and of course, everyone I saw wanted to know about the job.

In the cab itself, so many passengers always asked me, "So what's it like to be a female cab driver?" I found the question to be incredibly annoying, but I usually tried to humor them. By passenger number twenty, I would get sick of it and not say anything, or make some stupid snarky remark like, "A female? I'm a female? Shit. I had no idea. What's it like to be a male whatever-you-are?" Or I would say, "I don't know. I've never been a man before so I have nothing to compare it to." One elderly man, after hearing this answer, replied, "Well, there's still time."

And other times, I would simply say, "It's just like being a male cab driver except without a penis."

Out at the bar, it seemed like it was all people were interested in, and the worst part of it was, it seemed like it was all I really had in me to talk about anymore. A typical exchange that night included someone coming up, greeting Allie, and asking her about the TV show she was working on. Then they would turn to me and say, "So? You still driving?" At this, they would make the usual hands-on-the-steering-wheel gesture, moving them slightly right and left to indicate the act of driving. I would nod and say yes and then try to change the subject.

I felt a little guilty. I understood their curiosity, I really did, but I just could not bring myself to talk about it anymore. I no longer wanted to show off. Unless, of course, it was a cute girl doing the asking. Then all that reticence would disappear in a second. Unfortunately that wasn't the normal state of things. Instead, when someone asked how it was going or wanted me to tell them some "crazy stories," I would just respond with something vague and evasive like, "It's pretty routine. You know, it's a job." Then I would back out of the conversation with something like, "I'm gonna go get a drink. I'll be right back." What was I gonna say? "I'm miserable and hate it and feel like a total failure"? Or how about "I'm not strong enough or patient enough to do this job"? Or even "If I had to do this for the rest of my life, I might seriously consider suicide"? Yeah, that's a good conversation starter. Instead, I managed to avoid talking about it for most of the night and took refuge in Allie's closeness until finally it was time to go.

The scene altered itself only once that night, when an acquaintance, a girl named Alex, approached and, after going through the usual routine, said, "I'm actually thinking about doing it too. How hard is it to get the license?"

"Oh really?" I was a little surprised. Some small part of me felt a little proprietary jealousy, like I owned it or something. This was *my* thing, she couldn't copy me! As petty as it was, and as embarrassing as it is to admit, being the only cab driver in my circle of friends sometimes made me feel special and almost sort of cool, even though I was miserable and never wanted to talk about it. Still, I knew this was going to happen sooner or later.

I told her what she had to do to get her license, pointed her to the TLC website, where I had gotten all the necessary forms, and gave her some sort of tired discouragement. I said, "It's really hard, but maybe you'll be better at it than me." She probably really would've been. She liked people more, had more patience, and was more eager to talk and engage with strangers than I was. As long as she didn't get lost, Alex would probably make a great weirdo New York cabbie. Of course, she never did go through with any of it, so I never got to see how another young white college-educated dyke fared in the job.

When I went back to work a few days later, I tried to have a different mind-set. I was determined to maintain a positive yet realistic attitude, so I went to the garage hoping for the best but remembering to be prepared for the worst.

The season was already changing and the air felt crisp and charged. It was windy and cold, and the high clouds made the sky gray and overcast, yet still bright. It was my favorite kind of day. The few remaining ice cream trucks were sounding out their last gasps, their cheery jingles sounding more like death knells all around town. The fire hydrants had all been recapped and there were no longer any kids playing in the streets in their homemade water parks. People were coming back to town, getting down to business, going back to school.

And, as cheesy as it sounds, it really felt like something new was beginning, the change of season sort of bringing other changes along with it, offering up a new chance, even if it was only the beginning of another long, dark winter. There was a distinct undercurrent of excitement, and it felt like everyone wanted to stick close together. The lights inside the garage felt bright and warm, and it was as if we all suddenly realized how much we needed one another.

The waiting room was crowded with guys. Everyone was ready to work. Helen was already there, as were Stewie and Daniel and Rodrigo. Sometimes that happened, when everyone just showed up. It was part of that feeling in the air—a combination of the weather, the mood in the city, and the collective unconscious, when everyone has the exact same impulses at the same time, like when a restaurant is slow all night and then gets superbusy within a span of ten minutes.

Guys were milling about in little groups, waiting around for the day drivers to roll in. Judging from the crowd, I knew it would be a while before I got out. Not the best way to start a shift, but it wasn't the worst either. In fact, sometimes just hanging out there bullshitting with everyone was my favorite part of the day.

Daniel was involved in an intense two-player game of Ms.

Pac-Man, so I pulled up a chair next to Helen and Stewie in the waiting room.

A football game was blaring from the television. Stewie was fiddling with his new cell phone and Helen was reading the newspaper. She looked up and greeted me. "Hello, darling. And how are you today?"

"Eh. Okay, I guess. How are you?"

"I'm very good, actually. I have some news." She paused for dramatic affect, and then continued, "I think I'm going to be leaving here soon. I'm finally making my grand exit. There's a new tour bus company and I just went for my second interview. If all goes well, I should be a tour guide again in one month's time."

Stewie, who had clearly already heard Helen's big news, was concerned with his phone and kept interrupting us to ask how to get the speaker feature to work. "I don't get it. How do you use this *fakakta* thing?" he asked, using the Yiddish word for "shitty." He went on, "I'm gonna send it back. It's junk." Then to me, "Do you know how to use it? Here, see if you can figure it out." I took the phone and said to Helen, "Congratulations! That's great news."

"Yes, it most certainly is. But please keep it under your hat for now. I haven't told David yet."

Stewie piped in and asked me, "Do you know anything about knishes? My cousin knows a guy who distributes Gabila's knishes. We should go into business together and sell knishes and bagels."

I replied, "I *like* knishes, but other than that, no, I don't know much about them."

The door to the waiting room opened and Ricky hobbled in. As he plunked down on one of the benches near the window, his smell slowly started to fill the room. "Hello, Melissa. You gonna let me in the bathroom today? Leave it open when you come out."

I had decided I wasn't going to let Ricky use the women's room anymore. I'd let him in there too many times just to find he'd peed all over the floor and the toilet seat, hadn't flushed, and had left the poorly ventilated room stinking like stale old-man urine. It was too much. There was a men's room he could do that to. Plus, I had gotten into trouble for letting him in there.

"I can't do it anymore, Ricky. Paul found out about it and he threatened to take away my bathroom key if I let any guys in there. He said he didn't give a shit if I had to walk to the restaurant up the street to pee." Paul was mad because he used the women's room too, and didn't like the idea of Ricky using it. That bathroom was kept nice and clean since it was used only by the employees at the garage and the female drivers, of which there was usually a maximum of two or three at any given time. The 150 or so male drivers had to use, you know, the *men's* room.

Ricky stuck his lips out in a sort of pathetic pout and said, "Come on. You're not gonna work with me?"

I just replied, "Sorry, Ricky. I can't."

Helen observed this entire exchange and gave me a wink. Then, with an amused smile, she joked, "You should be letting *me* in that bathroom. At least I *look* the part."

Stewie chimed in with his usual corny-ass sense of humor, "You should let Ricky in if he wears a dress. Hey, Harvey, you should lend him something! I think it would fit." Everyone just sort of groaned.

I smiled back at Helen and said, "I'm definitely gonna miss you around here when you go. What am I gonna do with these guys without you?"

"Don't worry, honey. We're going to stay in touch."

I was still holding Stewie's phone, but it really was too confusing. I gave up trying to figure it out, handed it back to him, and went outside for a cigarette. The late autumn/early winter air made me feel reflective. I was thinking mainly about Helen. I was really happy for her. But I was a little sad for me. I had come to look forward to seeing her at the garage, and now she would be gone. I had found that once a person left the garage, it was difficult to maintain a friendship. Everyone had such different schedules, it just made it so much harder to coordinate. And besides, it was just easy to be friends with people you had to see each day before work. But I wanted to stay in touch with Helen, and I hoped it would really happen.

I got the cab at around 4:30 and made my way into the city. I needed a good night. I needed bad stuff to not happen. But most of all, I needed to stay calm and cool if I was going to make it through the shift.

I did okay. There were a few small challenges, mainly in the form of traffic and shitty drivers, but I survived without any meltdowns or accidents or major traumas. Nobody even gave me the finger that night, which was pretty remarkable.

There was one ride that I thought might get a little rocky. I picked up this Puerto Rican guy, and when he saw my hack license displayed on the back of the partition, he wanted to know the ethnic origin of my last name. When I told him it was German, he told me his girlfriend was German. I guess he didn't realize that someone could be German and Jewish at the same time, because he started going on about the Holocaust and how "the Jews should just stop whining about it already."

He said, "What's the point of continuing to bring it up? It happened, it's over, let it go already."

I kept my cool, and simply said, "It's important to keep telling the story so that it never happens again. If you forget and let it go, history has a tendency to repeat itself."

Then he said, "Yeah, but do you really think six million Jews died? I mean, come on. They've *got* to be exaggerating."

It was getting a little harder to stay calm. I took a deep, deep breath and replied, "I *do* believe it. I also happen to know that my grandmother fled Germany because she was Jewish. She came to New York when she was twenty-seven years old because things were so horrible over there. And most people in her family weren't so lucky. I don't think there's any exaggeration. It was an incredibly fucked-up moment in history and it's important to remember it, whether you're Jewish or not."

I wanted to go on, but I managed to stop myself from getting into a full-on rant. We weren't supposed to get into political or religious or any other kind of debates with our passengers. It never led to any good, and often led to them calling 311 and filing a complaint with the TLC. I had stayed as calm as I could manage, but, clearly, I had too personal a connection to this issue.

My passenger stayed quiet for a moment, and I wasn't sure if that was just the end of the conversation or what. But after a minute, he said, "You know, it's good when someone pulls your ear a little and educates you on stuff you don't really know about. You learn something. I guess I didn't realize how bad it really was."

He was being serious. I was actually a little shocked. I never would have expected this guy to be so open-minded. His reaction came as a surprise and a relief. The inside of the cab was a big part of my life, but to most passengers, it was just a passing moment. They're not always ready or willing to take me on as a moment in *their* lives—to have a real conversation with me that's not about driving the goddamn cab, and to give an actual shit about what I have to say.

Still, in this case, though I may have gone too far in terms of driver-passenger relations, he was a cool person, and he apparently got something out of my little rant.

When we reached his destination, he paid and got out, but not before actually *thanking* me for having that conversation with him.

Sometimes people can really surprise you.

I needed to start thinking about what would come next, to prepare for the next adventure. The problem was, I had no clue what it could be, and I was back to that same old dilemma of feeling stuck in something and not knowing exactly how to get out. It was around this time that I tried to cut down on my driving shifts and took a part-time job as a dog-walker. It didn't last. Though I loved the interaction with animals, being outside, and having a guaranteed (though quite small) paycheck, the six hours a day of walking was too much for my never-fully-healed left foot.

After three days, the pain was tremendous, and all the ice packs and Advils in the world couldn't make it go away. I called up on the fourth day and quit.

I continued driving the cab, and things were okay for a while. Sometimes it even felt like my passengers picked up on my vibe of "please don't mess with me, I'm too tired" and were extra nice, like the night when I was deep into my shift and got a fare to Brooklyn Heights. It was already past midnight but we got stuck in the usual screwed-up traffic on the FDR approach to the Brooklyn Bridge. For whatever reason, the NYPD seemed to think that placing two empty cop cars in the left lane at the entrance to the bridge was going to somehow act as a deterrent to terrorism. All it did, however, was create a long, slow-moving stream of tired and angry drivers that stretched all the way up the FDR to the Williamsburg Bridge, a mile away. I never saw the point of it.

So I was taking this guy over to Brooklyn and we got stuck

in the usual stupid backup. He was a lawyer, had been working until midnight and he was eager to get home.

We finally made it onto and over the bridge and were in his neighborhood when he informed me he had to stop at the bodega to get cash. This is usually annoying, when people get into a cab without money on them, but if it's late enough at night, it doesn't so much matter. We're not losing that much business anyway.

We stopped, and when he came back from the store, I saw he not only had gotten his cash, but he had bought me a fancy iced-tea drink with ginseng in it. He said he saw me yawning as we were sitting in all that bridge traffic, so he thought he'd get me a little pick-me-up, since I still had a few hours of work left.

I usually didn't accept things like food and drinks from passengers, but I made an exception this time because I really did need it, and because the gesture was so pure and well-intentioned. The only other time I accepted something like that from a passenger was when a family of Midwestern tourists offered me a pickled tomato from Guss' Pickles on the Lower East Side. That being one of my favorite foods ever, I couldn't say no. I ate the tomato after they got out, while pulled over in midtown, and it put me in a good mood for the rest of the night. The same went with this iced tea. It was the little things like this that kept me going.

The next few weeks went by relatively smoothly. People got in, I drove them somewhere, and they paid me. It was that simple. On one occasion, I drove two dominatrices (dominatrixes? dominatrii?) to the Upper West Side while one of them, whose head was shaved entirely bald, carried on a lengthy cell phone conversation. She was discussing which classes she should teach at an upcoming fetish festival, and I assumed she was some sort of bondage specialist because a few of the classes she mentioned included Intro to Japanese Rope Bondage, Rope for Couples, and, my personal favorite, Erotic Macramé.

They were making two stops and the cell phone talker got out first. Once we were alone together heading up Amsterdam, the remaining passenger began a conversation. It started with the usual, "So, a female cab driver. Do you ever get scared?" I replied with one of my many canned answers, this time keeping it short and polite, simply saying, "No. I'm only afraid of accidents," before turning it around and asking, "And what do *you* do?"

"I'm a dominatrix."

Then she continued, "Well, I usually don't tell people that right away, but I figured after hearing that conversation my friend just had in here, there aren't any secrets left between us."

"At this point, it takes quite a bit to surprise me," I said. "In fact, I'd rather have a dominatrix in my cab than some shitty Wall Street banker. They're so boring."

At this, she said, "Oh my God, I hate those guys! They book appointments with me and then act like they own me because they're paying me. I always have to teach them a lesson and show them who's in charge. But the sad thing is, that's how they treat everyone. They're so pathetic and disgusting, but at least I get to abuse them a little. Unfortunately, I'm still doing what they want me to do."

"You shouldn't take appointments with them anymore."

"I don't really have a choice. I need the money. If there were more regular, normal clients, I would definitely limit the Wall Street guys, but they make up a big chunk of my clientele."

"Actually, I know what you mean. It's the same with the cab. Sometimes they'll get in and not even tell me where to go. They'll just continue talking on their precious little cell phones, having the most important conversation in the world, and, you know, because they think they're the masters of the universe, I should just automatically know where they're going. And when I have to interrupt them to get the destination, they act like I just did the most annoying thing in the world. It's so fucking irritating. I hate those guys with such a passion. And they always tip for shit."

"Tell me about it."

"I'd rather have dominatrices and escorts—or even hookers and pimps—in my cab over those guys any day of the week."

With that, we arrived at a nice building where a doorman hurried to the curb to help her out of the cab. She tipped me generously and went inside.

Things were getting better. I was getting better. My confidence was returning and even my patience was improving. I was starting to almost enjoy the job, or at least talking to the passengers who weren't assholes.

I continued to have a good run for a while. A few nights later, I picked up four people in the Meatpacking District who were going to a club called Stereo in Chelsea. When the fourth passenger was getting in the front seat next to me, I sort of snapped at him because he almost sat on my jacket before I had a chance to move it out of the way.

He said, "Are you having a bad night?" I replied, "Not really. I just don't want your butt on my jacket." Luckily these people were all in high spirits, so they said, "Don't worry. We're gonna tip you really well. In fact, we're gonna make your night." I figured I'd believe it when I saw it, and just said, "Sure, okay."

When we got to the club, the fare was five dollars. The guy sitting next to me handed me a fifty and told me to keep the change. Then he said, "See? I *told* you we were gonna make your night!" I held up the fifty in disbelief and thanked him. Then he said, "*Now* can I sit on your jacket?"

He was right. They did pretty much make my night. Big tips have that effect. It must have something to do with those Chelsea clubs.

While I ended up having a pretty lucky night, one of my later passengers *got* lucky. He was the male half of a boy-girl couple I picked up in SoHo. They were two young white almost-yuppies, but they seemed nice enough. It was clear that they had a few drinks in them and were warmed up to each other, but when they got in, the girl said they were making two stops. That's a sad date-ender from the guy's perspective, I'm sure, but he played it very cool and, quite wisely, insisted on dropping the girl off at her place first even though his apartment was closer. They spent the entire ride making out heavily in the backseat.

When we finally reached her building, the guy's chivalry paid off as she uttered those six magic words: "Do you want to come up?"

He shoved the money at me before I even had a chance to shut the meter off, and couldn't get out of the cab fast enough.

CHAPTER 18

That December, the transit workers went on strike to fight for a better contract from the MTA. All subways and city buses were out of commission for three days, and the five boroughs were in a state of chaos. Those three days turned out to be the coldest that winter.

There was a lot of tension leading up to it, and I had mixed feelings about the idea of driving a cab through the strike. It was a tricky thing because, in an informal, unspoken way, it was seen almost as scabbing against the transit workers, even though cab drivers ultimately had nothing to do with them and we weren't even unionized ourselves. But the transit workers wanted to show their impact on the city, to demonstrate how valuable they were, and thirteen thousand cabs driving stranded New Yorkers around could potentially lessen that effect, even if only by the tiniest of amounts.

I felt a small degree of solidarity with transit workers despite all the angry, homicidal bus drivers I had encountered along the way. I wasn't entirely dependent on public transportation since I had the Buick, but I certainly took the subway and buses enough to appreciate them. And my allegiance to transit employees was only strengthened whenever one of them actually did something nice for me, like when a conductor would hold the subway doors open for me as I was running to catch the train.

My dilemma was that the strike presented a unique opportunity for me and my fellow cab drivers to make some serious cash, since demand for taxis would be at an unprecedented high. I was in no position to say no to extra money, but I also knew that all the extra traffic would probably balance things out to some degree, making the work not as lucrative as some cabbies might hope.

Coincidentally, I had just finished reading a book I found in a thrift store, called *Underground Woman* by Marian Swerdlow. She was one of the first female subway conductors in New York, working for Transit from 1982 to 1986. She eventually left the job because she got so sick of being regularly assaulted by angry passengers.

The book gave a real inside look at how the MTA and the Transport Workers Union (TWU) operated in the early eighties, and even included an account of a slowdown enacted by the transit workers to protest the dangerous and decaying conditions of the tracks and trains, which were in a state of disrepair left over from the seventies. Swerdlow's book gave me a new perspective on transit workers, so it was really difficult not to side with them. But I also had to wonder, if the situation had been reversed and cabbies were actually unionized and were threatening to strike (oh, say for an eight-hour workday instead of twelve, or for health benefits, or a pension plan, or felony protection from assault, none of which we currently have, and all of which the transit workers have), would the transit workers act in solidarity with *us*? I doubted it.

But that wasn't the point. The point was, the city wanted to use its thirteen thousand cabs to try to counter the effects of the strike, to show the transit union the workers weren't that necessary after all, that the city could survive without them if need be. This was made clear by all the newspaper articles and Taxi and Limousine Commission posters that were up at the garage instructing us on how to handle the strike, thanking us for helping the city, and, most important, hinting at how much money we could make.

I never met a cabbie who wasn't broke or struggling, so this approach was well targeted. I knew some guys who would sit out the strike simply because the huge amount of traffic would probably give them a heart attack, but I also knew that many cabbies would work in the hopes of making enough money to carry them through the slow-business month of January. And without our own union, it was, like always, every man for himself.

Like I said, it was a tricky situation.

The strike took effect early on the Tuesday morning five days before Christmas, right in the middle of the big holiday shopping season. When I woke up that morning and learned the strike was on, I deliberated whether or not I was truly prepared to deal with it. Traffic would be hell. People would be pissed. I might not make enough money. Plus, it was a Tuesday.

Over the previous few months, however, my confidence had returned. I had more patience and I was handling myself better in trying situations. Maybe the Tuesday hex could be lifted for this special occasion. I admit, I kinda just wanted to be a part of it. To see the city from a cab driver's perspective during this unique moment in New York history, to pitch in and help out, and, of course, to make some money.

I figured no amount of cabs could lessen the TWU's impact, so I decided not to feel guilty about that. I also decided the Tuesday hex was rendered powerless during the strike and I realized I couldn't miss this shift. I figured I'd call David at the garage, and if he could actually spare me a cab, I would work.

Since a lot of cabbies couldn't get to the garage without the subway, there were plenty of cabs available and I was able to capitalize on the big event because of the Buick. When David assigned me a cab, he also handed me a sheet of paper issued by the Taxi and Limousine Commission, as well as a photocopied newspaper article, both of which detailed the temporary "zone system" and flat rates we would be using. We were not to run the meter. Instead, we were instructed to pick up as many passengers as possible—up to four—and charge the new city-mandated rates, per person, depending on where they were going. The city was divided into zones for this purpose, and we were provided with a crudely drawn map so we could know where each one started and ended.

I got in the cab, crossed the 59th Street Bridge, and entered the mayhem.

I realized right away, with my first cab-full of fares, that my job that night was going to be primarily about route coordination. In order to not go in every different direction, I had to stop and ask each passenger which way they were heading before they got into the cab. This pissed off a whole lot of people standing on the streets, but it was absolutely necessary. Otherwise the people already in the cab would get upset, and rightfully so, especially if they had to go forty blocks out of the way just because you picked someone up who was going in the totally opposite direction. Of course, not everyone's destination was perfectly on the way, so there were lots of people jumping out on compromised corners and walking the remaining one or two blocks to where they needed to go. There were only a very small number of passengers who were unhappy with this arrangement, but I guess that was my fault for not recognizing that these people were the most important people in the world.

Overall, that first night of the strike, most of the passengers I picked up were great. They were willing to work with one another's destinations and tried to help me plan the best routes. Many of them even got to know one another along the way.

During rush hour especially, when things on the streets were the most hectic, my cab was filled with lively conversations as passengers offered one another tips and opinions on how to get around town for the duration of the strike. With strangers all hanging out, talking about their jobs and their bosses, about the mayor, about their kids, it was one of those "only in New York" days that are so rare, yet so cool when they actually happen. It was like a big New York family reunion, involving every single person in the city. The only other times I'd ever experienced anything like that were during the weeks following September 11, 2001, and during the blackout of August 2003.

Despite the many challenging traffic moments of that night, I was able to keep my cool. Most people were in good spirits, savoring the novelty of the strike—at least for the first day— and thanking me for taking them home. I felt like the host of a big party that was happening in my backseat, and everyone was invited.

Of course, there's always a weirdo or two thrown into every shift for good measure, and strike night was no exception. Filling the quota for that shift, my strangest fare got in around midnight, when traffic cooled down and business got a little sparse. I was cruising the Lower East Side when I picked him up. He was going to the main Hare Krishna temple on Schermerhorn and Nevins in Brooklyn. After talking for a while about his spiritual beliefs, and after handing me about four different Krishna-related business cards, he said, "It was not just a coincidence that you picked me up tonight."

But, not to bust his little Krishna bubble or anything, it *was* just a coincidence. You know what, it wasn't even a *coincidence*. It was just my job, nothing more, nothing less. I mean, seriously, I'll pick up whoever hails me, usually from thirty to forty people on a normal night, and it is never because the universe specially orchestrated it. It's just because I was there and they were there, and I had room in my cab and I needed to make money. On the other hand, luck—blind, meaningless, dumb luck—does have something to do with it, but that has no relationship with any greater purposes. It's just what it is: luck.

Anyway, this guy continued telling me his entire life story and eventually revealed that he used to deal hash to high school students when he was younger. He went on to say that he had spent a little time in jail for his crimes before he found Krishna.

Not one minute after that, as he was telling me how he was into food and cooking and stuff, he handed me a little ball of chocolate wrapped in foil and informed me it was infused with all sorts of "special herbs and spices." I figured it was impolite to refuse it, so I took it and put it in my pocket, knowing I would not be tasting it anytime soon.

The next night, I was hanging out at Allie's when the ball fell out of my sweatshirt pocket and onto her couch. But I didn't realize this until much later the following day. I called her up in a panic and left a spazzed-out message, saying, "If you find a chocolate ball on your couch, DO NOT EAT IT. It is from a passenger of mine and he was a totally sketchy Hare Krishna guy. I repeat: DO NOT EAT THE CHOCOLATE BALL."

Allie, luckily, had not noticed the candy in her couch. When she finally found it after hearing my insane message, she decided she needed to keep the chocolate ball forever. To this day, the foil-wrapped chocolate sits intact and uneaten in the pencil holder on Allie's desk.

That first night of the strike, I noticed that the city buses had been taken over by the NYPD. There were tons of them all over town and they all had signs taped over the MTA logo that said NYPD VEHICLE. At one point, I was stopped at a light across the street from one heading in the opposite direction, and the cop behind the wheel grinned big and threw me the peace sign.

He was the second cop that night who had been really friendly to me. Earlier in the evening a police cruiser rolled up next to me and the cops inside volunteered all this information about the chaos that was going down at Penn Station. They were all smiles and even gave me a thumbs-up.

This, in my experience, was unprecedented behavior. You know things are weird in New York when the police are all loving on taxi drivers.

I went home that night with a nice wad of cash in my pocket, more than I had ever made in a single shift, but despite my success, I wimped out of working Wednesday night. As the strike went into its second day, more people decided to brave the streets and drive into Manhattan. Traffic reached a level of hell that was unusual even for New York, with accounts of drivers sitting on the same block for up to an hour without moving, and so, naturally, the vibe on the streets grew increasingly edgy.

I had been hearing all these news reports about cabbies upping the fares, which I found troublesome. However, the mayor addressed this issue in a press conference on Wednesday, and I was relieved to hear him say that he believed many of the complaints were coming from people who were unfamiliar with the temporary zone-pricing system the city had enforced for the duration of the strike.

Indeed, most of my passengers that Tuesday night had no idea about the rate changes, and I found myself explaining it over and over again. Many people, when informed of the price to their destination, opted to try their luck with a different cab, but I'm sure they never got quoted a lower price than what I was offering, since I was going strictly by the book (or, rather, that sheet of paper that was distributed by the garage, which had been issued by the city).

Only one woman I had in the cab was particularly rude and pissed off about the price I charged her. I picked her up around 80th Street and West End Avenue. I'd seen her talking to the driver of a cab in front of me, but she waved him away and flagged me down. That type of behavior was usually bad news, but for those few days, all the old logic was out the window.

She had a kid with her who must've been around twelve years old. When I pulled up, she said, "Will you take me to 105th and West End and not charge for my son? The cab I took down did it." There was already a tone of accusation in her voice, but I felt a little sorry for her, so I agreed. When they got in, I told her it was going to cost fifteen dollars since she was going into a different zone from the one I had picked her up in. The pricing system was such that it cost ten dollars to go anywhere within one zone and five dollars more for each additional zone entered, per person.

This pissed her off and she said, "The cab I took down only charged me ten. What the hell?"

I replied, "I'm just going by what the city says. I didn't make up the prices."

I offered to show her the paper with the new fares on it, but she refused to look at it, saying, "Yeah, whatever. It seems like every cab driver says something different. You guys obviously just charge whatever you want."

Now *I* was mad. I certainly wasn't trying to rip anyone off and she was implying that I was some sort of scam artist trying to swindle her out of five fucking dollars. I turned around and said, "Lady, I'm letting your kid ride for free. He's taking up a seat in my cab, which would make me more money if I could fill it. You're getting a bargain, if you ask me."

This effectively shut her up.

What was funny about this situation was that, earlier at the garage one of the conversations between drivers centered around whether or not a child "counts as a person," and whether or not we should charge for them to ride in our cabs. In the eyes of the NYPD, a kid counted as a passenger, and so they allowed a car with three adults and one child to drive in the temporary HOV4 zones that were instituted during the strike. But as far as these new taxi rates were concerned, we weren't so sure.

I figured if a kid was small enough to fit on their parent's lap, I wouldn't charge for them, and in other cases, I would just use my best judgment as to what seemed appropriate and fair. Luckily, this was the only time I'd had to deal with this situation so far, but unfortunately, the mother turned out to be an unappreciative piece of shit. I decided that, from then on, I would let kids ride for free, but their mothers would have to fucking WALK.

Scared off from working Wednesday night, I came up with the harebrained idea that I would work the Thursday morning shift instead, thinking the traffic would be lighter. I wanted to get an early start and get into the city by 3:00 A.M. in an attempt to avoid the major crush of cars that would try to cross the bridges and tunnels starting at 4:00. My sleep schedule was so adjusted to working the night shift that I ended up just staying awake all day and night, relaxing on Allie's couch, drinking Red Bull, and watching TV until it was time to go.

When I got into Manhattan, business was slow until around 7:30, when the real rush hour began. By then, though, people were already sick of the strike, and they were taking it out on us cab drivers. They were mad that they had to pay more than the cost of a subway or bus fare to get to work, they were mad that it was still so cold outside, and they were mad they couldn't get their holiday shopping done.

We were no longer in this together and people started arguing with me about the fares I was charging, again accusing me of trying to rip them off, threatening not to pay, and basically acting like assholes. Apparently, over the past few days, no one had really paid attention to the countless articles in all the papers about how taxis were operating under the new strike regulations. And my feeling was, if you don't want to pay, don't take a cab. Period. But there were many people with that old sense of entitlement, and all of a sudden, the huge gulf between me and my white-collar passengers became glaringly apparent all over again. We were not equals. Our New York solidarity had completely evaporated. Now I was merely at their service, and also at their mercy. They could curse at and argue with and abuse me to their hearts' delight, and if I dared make a peep in my own defense, they had 311—the New York City complaint line—on speed-dial.

The constant reminders of my inferiority to all these lawyers and bankers and advertising executives, plus my lack of sleep for the previous twenty-four hours, drained me of all energy. Even Red Bull could not pick me back up. By eleven o'clock Thursday morning, I was a wreck. There was still business, but I knew that if I continued working, I would probably have an accident. Money didn't matter anymore. I just needed to sleep. I hit my off-duty light and headed toward the Williamsburg Bridge, figuring it was my best bet out of Manhattan.

As I took my place in traffic on the bridge, an announcement came over the radio that the MTA and the TWU, with the help of state mediators, had reached an agreement. By the end of the day, the strike would be over. I could almost feel the entire city breathe a sigh of relief.

Two hours later, I finally made it back to my apartment. I was unconscious the second I hit the bed and didn't get up until the following afternoon. The strike was over. I had survived.

CHAPTER 19

It took over two years but the settlement check from my accident finally came through. Of course the lawyers got a third of it, but it was more money than I had had in my bank account in a long time. I couldn't deposit it fast enough, and I immediately set about the important task of working less.

I had already been cutting down on my shifts, but now I made special plans to work as little as possible for as long as I could. I couldn't live off the settlement check for too long, so I still had to work at least one or two days a week. But things had also changed. I didn't feel so defeated by the job anymore, and I wasn't going as crazy as often. Of course, it still never stopped being stressful. One Thursday night in particular, I was especially tested, and I felt proud of myself for being able to keep my head on straight.

I had been stuck out at LaGuardia Airport for an hour before I finally got a passenger arriving from Chicago at around 1:00 A.M. On our approach to the Grand Central Parkway entrance ramp, I heard police sirens. I slowed down and looked around but didn't see any lights. Assuming the sound was coming from the highway, I continued on.

As I was about to take the right turn onto the ramp, I noticed a huge white SUV barreling down the street from the other direction. He was heading my way, but I didn't think anything of it. The sirens were louder by then so I just sort of assumed that this driver was politely getting out of the way for the cops. This thought continued for another second until I saw the SUV cross over into the oncoming traffic lane and jump onto the entrance ramp behind me just as I was completing my turn. A police car and an undercover cop in a taxi (many precincts have yellow cabs that they use as undercover vehicles) were speeding after him with their lights flashing and sirens blaring.

At this point, I realized the SUV was not trying to get out of the way *for* the cops, but rather, he was trying to get away *from* the cops. He was bearing down on me, but there was no place for me to go since it was just a little one-lane ramp with medium-size curbs on each side. Not wanting to get rammed out of the way by the clearly desperate fugitive behind me, I slowed down as much as I could and tried to get my cab onto the curb without blowing a tire.

The SUV was up my ass, and the second I got over enough to give him room, he gunned it and blew past me, the cops hot on his tail. I paused for a second and then carefully pulled the car back onto the ramp and watched as they all shot west down the Grand Central Parkway toward the city. When my heart finally started beating again, I turned to my passenger and said, "Welcome to New York!"

And, just like that, we laughed and it was okay. I mean, I had been scared, but I didn't freak out or have a meltdown or anything. Something had definitely changed in me.

A few weeks later, on the Sunday of the Gay Pride Parade, I thought for sure I would get good tips. I figured the gays would recognize me as one of their own and would somehow congratulate me for being a gay cab driver or something. As it turned out, not one homosexual I picked up that night took a second look at me, and their tips were standard.

My first passenger of the day was actually a straight married guy named Steve. He was going to the Museum of Modern Art on 53rd Street. A short ride, nothing out of the ordinary.

I was in a good mood, so I started up a conversation. "You going to see something special there today?" I asked.

"Not really," he answered. "I'm just meeting my son there. He just graduated from NYU and we're spending the day together."

Traffic was light and the trip only took about seven minutes, but during that time, we actually broke through the surface of our complete-stranger-ness and learned something about each other. When he asked me how and why I'd started driving a cab, something about his approach was different from all the other people who'd asked me those questions a thousand times before. It was clear he wasn't really surprised, and he wasn't marveling at me for being a female cab driver. It was almost like he'd seen it all before and he just sort of *got it*. And suddenly I found myself being sincere and honest, ditching the usual sarcastic shtick that helped me cope with the "job interview" part of my job.

I tried to summarize it for him. "I don't really know why I'm doing it anymore. I mean, I guess I still need the money but it started out as an adventure. I decided somewhere along the way that I wanted to have as many adventures and experiences as possible, and this was the first one on the list."

I saw his eyes smile in the rearview mirror and he started telling me about all the adventures he had when he was younger. "I traveled all over the world, worked on an oil rig for a while, went to Alaska, then down to Argentina." He paused for a second, seemingly lost in memory, then said, "I had no idea what I was *supposed* to be doing, but I can tell you this: Sometimes I really miss those days."

"What do you do now?"

"I'm a money manager."

"Oh."

After a moment, he said, "So what's your next step? What will your next adventure be?"

"I'm still not sure," I said. "I have such a hard time picking just one thing. I sort of started writing again, but I don't know exactly where that's going. I really just don't want to get stuck in anything."

We pulled up in front of the museum and the meter read $4.10. He sat in the back for a second, counting out his money. Then he handed me seven $20 bills and said, "Here's a hundred and forty dollars. Don't give up."

I took the money and stared at it in disbelief.

"Are you serious?" I almost went to hand it back to him. This had to be a mistake.

"Yes," he looked at me meaningfully. *"Don't give up."*

He went to open the door.

I felt my eyes well up with tears, but I didn't cry. I just looked at him as he was getting out and said, *"Thank you."*

"No problem," he said, and smiled. Then he shut the door and walked into the museum to meet his son.

It is a moment I will never forget.

■   ■   ■

Even though things seemed to be getting a little better, I still wasn't totally reformed from my crazy, stressed-out, selfish cabbie behavior. Not too long after that night, I was on the Upper East Side in the middle of rush hour. The city was busy and everything was going smoothly when I pulled up to the light at 79th and First Avenue. I saw a guy get out of a cab on the block ahead and start walking my way with his hand in the air, trying to hail another cab. Something about him, maybe the luggage he was carrying, or maybe the fact that he'd just gotten *out* of a cab, made me want to not pick him up.

The light was red and he was at least half a block up, far enough away that I could've pretended like I didn't see him, and I told myself, *When the light turns green, turn up First Avenue. Don't pick this guy up. He's either trouble or he's going to the airport.*

But for some reason, despite my better judgment, when the light changed, I went straight. *Maybe he's going to Penn Station.* I pulled over, and after putting the luggage in the trunk, he sat down in the back and said, "LaGuardia."

I could've kicked myself. It was 5:15. Deep rush hour. This was the time to make your money in the city, not the time to leave and get screwed at the airport. But what was I gonna do? I just sucked it up and headed toward the Triborough Bridge.

On the way, somewhere high up on Third Avenue, traffic got a little tight and people were honking. A car nearby honked at me when I was trying to change lanes. It's something that happens all the time and to everyone, but this guy didn't seem to think so. At that moment, he said, "How long have you been a cab driver?"

Something in his tone of voice told me he wasn't just asking out of curiosity. It sounded more accusatory, like he wanted to school me or something. I was already annoyed that I had to take him to the airport during rush hour, and now he was asking me this question with an attitude, so I answered, "Thirty years."

It was obvious that this was a joke, since I was thirty years old at the time and looked much younger than my age. But he didn't seem to find it very funny. Instead, he just stared at me in the rearview.

I continued, "Why do you want to know?"

With an obnoxious tone in his voice, he replied, "I just don't want to get killed, that's all."

I felt a surge of heat rush to my cheeks, and said, "And why do you think you're gonna get killed?"

He said, "Because everyone's honking at you."

I spoke slowly, like a third-grade teacher, and said, "No, actually, *one* person honked at me. It's something that happens quite often and to most drivers, not just me. People honk quite liberally around here, if you haven't noticed."

He answered, "Okay, fine, one person honked. I just don't want to get killed."

I said, "If you don't like the way I'm driving, you can get out here. I won't charge you."

But he replied, "Well, I'm not gonna get out *here.*" We were in Harlem by then. "I'll never get another cab."

I offered to take him back to 79th Street free of charge, but he declined that as well. So I said, "Fine. Whatever. But tell me something. Do you think you would've said something like that to me if I was a man?"

He answered, "Yeah, I would've. I got out of a cab back on Seventy-ninth Street because the guy was being an asshole."

When he said this, I realized he was one of those passengers who would not be satisfied with their cab driver no matter what they did. Then he repeated yet again that he didn't want to get killed, and that's when I snapped and said, "Well, if you don't want to die, you got in the wrong cab, because I *do* want to die. And guess what? I've decided that today's the day."

I think, at this, he got the point. He put his hands up in a conciliatory gesture and said, "Okay, okay, I get it. I'm sorry. Let's just talk about something else. . . . What kind of music do you like?"

We spent the rest of the ride talking about bands and stuff. He told me how he liked "fucked-up music, like Kittie and Bio-hazard." And when I asked him what he did for a living, he said he was a "skin doctor."

I said, "Like, a dermatologist?"

"Uh, yeah." I think he thought "skin doctor" sounded cooler or something.

He was a dermatologist who liked hard music and he didn't want to die.

When we arrived at the terminal, the fare was $27.10. The skin doctor said, "I'm sorry I was such a dick back there. Will forty dollars make it up to you?" I thought for half a second and said, yes, $40 would help. He gave me the two twenties, thanked me profusely, and got out.

I was starting to become aware of just how much I had changed—or, rather, how much the job had changed me. This became very clear one night that summer on Flatbush Avenue.

I was on my way back to Manhattan after dropping off a fare in Park Slope, Brooklyn, and was chatting on the phone with Rodrigo. It was illegal for cabbies to talk on the phone while driving, even on a hands-free device, but everyone did it anyway. I had my own rules about never doing it while I had a passenger, but at that moment, I was alone in the cab, so I was catching up with Rodrigo, trading stories about our nights. Flying down Flatbush toward the Manhattan Bridge, I saw some ambulances and police cars in the middle of the street a block ahead.

As I approached the scene, I saw a girl lying on the ground, being frantically attended to by EMTs. A few yards down, there was a mangled bicycle. And a little farther down from that, the cops were talking to a driver standing near a dented car, hazard lights flashing.

I passed slowly and there was a break in our conversation as I commented to Rodrigo, "Oh shit, someone went down on a bike on Flatbush. It doesn't look good."

The only thing that really caught his attention was my location.

"You're in Brooklyn?"

"Yeah."

And then we moved on to other topics.

CHAPTER 20

Helen had gone back to tour-guiding, but we still talked every few weeks or so. She left me a message near the end of that summer, and when I returned her call a few days later, she was laid up in bed. Of all the ironies in the world, Helen had experienced one of the sharpest. She had been crossing the street in midtown, on her way to work at the tour bus company, when she got hit by a cab. She went down, and onlookers rushed to her aid, but the cabbie was already gone.

If anyone understood this driver's actions, it was Helen. In her tenure driving the cab, she'd had more accidents than anyone else in the history of our garage, although she had been fortunate enough to never hit a pedestrian. Luckily, she wasn't hurt too badly. When I spoke to her, she was all doped up on Vicodin and waiting to hear the results from an MRI, but she remained in good spirits. She told me her ex-junkie daughter had moved in with her and seemed to be struggling but doing okay. She also told me she had plans, when she got back on her feet, to go over to the gay and lesbian center in Chelsea to see about getting on female hormones so she could have a chance of passing as a woman even just a tiny bit. We made vague plans to meet up for a drink sometime in a few weeks, after she healed up.

All the chaos of the previous months seemed to finally be dying down and things were going okay for me. My parents, though still not totally thrilled, were finally coming around to accepting the idea of me, their younger daughter, as a cab driver. My mom had started sending me newspaper clippings in the mail whenever she read an article that had something to do with the taxi industry. Of course, most of these clippings came from the metro crime briefings about cabbies getting attacked or robbed, and sometimes the clips consisted of scathing "exposés" by the *New York Post* trashing "the city's ten worst cabbies," or some other fine journalism like that. But every now and then there'd be a heartwarming little story about a brave or honest cabbie who'd done something amazingly good.

My dad did similar things, including making sure to tape the New York episode of *Taxicab Confessions* for me, and also finally giving up on the idea of me becoming a teacher. Instead, his main concerns became making fun of me for not working full-time, figuring out how I was going to pay for health insurance, and making sure I was saving enough money to pay my taxes at the end of the year. They both still worried a lot and thought the job was too dangerous, but in the end, I think they were actually a little proud of me.

I suspect my parents finally came around when they realized that, ultimately, it was a good thing for me to become a cab driver. I had stopped being so miserable and misdirected, had taken control of my life, and had gone out and *done* something. I was a happier person because of it, and they could see that. Despite all the struggle and strife of the job—and all the complaining and whining I never failed to do about it—I was much more content doing this shitty, screwed-up job than I'd ever been before in my life.

I thought my grasp on the job had finally sort of evened out and stabilized. And shortly before my thirty-first birthday, when I showed up at the garage, nearly two years after I'd started, everything was the same as it always was. Paul the crazy Romanian dispatcher threatened that he was going to leave his wife for me, Daniel was playing Ms. Pac-Man, Stewie was on the phone with LaGuardia Airport checking their cab status, and Rodrigo was still home, sleeping off his shift from the night before. I waited around a while until Paul gave me a cab and I started the night.

I was only an hour into my shift when a guy in a maroon Volvo pulled up next to me, stopped his car in the middle of traffic, and got out. He started screaming at me from the passenger side, and I gathered that I had done something with my driving that really pissed him off. I couldn't hear him so well because I had the AC on and the windows were closed. I had passengers: two twentysomething girls on their way to the Chinatown bus back to Boston, where they were from.

Cars were all backed up at a red light and I was stuck there, unable to move and trying to just ignore the guy, when he suddenly reeled back and punched my passenger-side window. It didn't break or anything, but it was a hard enough hit to get my full attention. Now I was a little nervous. The light stayed red for what seemed like forever. No one was moving. There was no escape route.

After he punched the window, he reached into the front of his pants. And this was when I really started to get scared, as I thought he might be reaching for a gun. I sat there frozen in my seat and thought, *Fuck. Okay, I guess this is really it,* but then I saw that, instead of a gun, he pulled out his penis.

He held it there for a second, in all its shriveled glory. Then he shook it a little, I guess to further drive home his point.

There I was, in broad daylight on the Bowery, buckled in behind the wheel of my cab, looking at a penis not four feet away. I was relieved that I wasn't about to be shot, but also horrified now in a totally different way, and there was a moment when the only thought that registered in my head was, *I can't believe this is my job.*

The girls in the back started freaking out, and to be honest, so did I.

After a moment, the guy put his penis away and walked back to his Volvo. The light turned green.

The two girls were really upset, and one of them said, "I can't believe that just happened. Are you gonna call the cops?"

I had learned by then that calling the cops was a big waste of time, but I did it anyway. I got a traffic agent on the street to make the Volvo pull over and wait for the squad car to come.

Of course, when the cops finally showed up fifteen minutes later, they did nothing. They didn't even give him a ticket.

I was pretty upset. The whole thinking-I-was-gonna-get-shot thing shook me up enough on its own, but then the dick thing plus the typical unhelpful-cops thing frustrated me and screwed with my head so much that I realized after dropping the Boston girls off that I needed to stop driving for the night.

More than anything, I was frustrated by my utter helplessness and powerlessness. I was pissed off about the second-class citizen status that is assigned to you the second you sit behind the wheel of a yellow cab, no matter what race, sex, nationality, or color you are. And what struck me the most about this was that it was probably what most nonwhite, non-American-born people experienced on a daily basis, and for the first time in my life, I was experiencing just the very tip of that iceberg. I remembered what Mike the American Eagle had told me nearly two years earlier: "Once you get behind the wheel of that cab, you lose all your rights. It's like you're not even American anymore."

I was pissed off by the cops and their refusal to take me seriously. And I was pissed off that some man thought it was okay to shove his penis at me because I was a woman, or a cab driver, or both.

But I also knew by then, that was the deal. It was just how it was.

When I got back to the garage, Omar the cashier was there—thank God it wasn't Paul—and in an attempt to cheer me up, he told me how two other drivers had been attacked through their windows just that past week. One ended up in the hospital and the other got away with just a punch to the face. A former cabbie himself, Omar said, "You'll never see people like you see them when you're driving a cab. It's the worst thing in the world."

Cabbies are cursed at and assaulted by the public on a daily basis, so I was very aware that the abuse wasn't directed only at me—but the penises sure did seem to be.

Maybe that should've been my answer when people asked me what it was like to be a "female cab driver."

A few days later, I saw Stewie at the garage. When I told him the story, he said, "We gotta get out of this business. . . . Wait, I got a job for you!"

I said, "Yeah? What?"

He got excited in his childlike way and started nudging my shoulder with the back of his hand like he always did. "There was an ad yesterday in *The Jewish Press*. You can be a ticket-taker at the heliport on Thirty-fourth Street!"

It was another one of his weird ideas, like the time he suggested we should go into the knish business together. I just said, "No thanks, I think I'd rather do something else."

Stewie pressed on. "Are you sure? I'll bring you the ad tomorrow."

When I declined again, he said, "Okay, I got a better idea. You know Woodbury Common, the outlet mall upstate?"

I was hesitant. "Yeah . . . I grew up sort of near there."

"Okay, well there's another place just like that in Pennsylvania. My cousin works there selling pretzels. My mother bought one and she couldn't believe the price he was charging. He's making a mint! Selling pretzels!"

Stewie was always coming up with something.

I smiled and nodded, knowing that, despite all his dreams, schemes, and ideas, Stewie would never leave the taxi business.

Knowing it wasn't the beginning of the rest of my life or anything, I started thinking more and more seriously about my next step. I started poking around on the Internet to see if I could find something there. A friend of mine had recently joined the fire department and encouraged me to sign up and take the test. I was interested and would have seriously considered it, but then I found out the FDNY only accepts new firefighters under the age of thirty. I was out of luck. But that led me to think about volunteering for the Red Cross. It seemed like a step toward becoming an animal cop somehow, so I decided to look into their disaster response courses and see what that was like.

Using (or, as my dad would say, "wasting") my settlement money, I was able to take extended breaks from driving here and there so I could immerse myself in other things. After one particularly long hiatus, when I hadn't driven a cab in nearly a month, I ran into another part-timer from my garage at a burger joint on Sixth Avenue.

He looked at me and said, "Where do I know you from?"

I recognized him immediately and said, "Crosstown, the taxi garage."

"Oh yeah! How's it going? Man, I haven't driven a cab in ages."

"Really? Me either. What are you up to these days?"

I remembered he was a photographer, and he explained that he was doing darkroom work at an office in the area. It sounded like a step up.

We chatted for a few minutes, and as we were parting ways, he paused for a second and said, "You know, as tough as that job is, I still miss it sometimes. Especially the freedom, of being out there." He motioned outside toward the street. "Now I'm stuck in an office with a boss, and it's easier, but it's not the same."

I watched all the cabs streak past out the window and said, "Yeah. I know what you mean."

I'd been off for a month, but all of a sudden, I felt myself missing the excitement of being in the cab. I felt the old impulse again, that familiar draw, and I knew I'd be back in the driver's seat again soon. The fact was, I could never completely quit. Despite everything, I *still* wasn't totally done with this adventure. I don't know if I ever will be.

I'll always keep my hack license current and up-to-date, renewing it every two years as required. I realized that if I stopped driving completely, I'd miss this crazy job a lot more than I'd ever anticipated. I'd miss the city and the chance to drop in on it and find out what it's really been up to, to catch up with it like an old friend I haven't seen or spoken to in a while.

Even now, whenever I'm not working, I'm still obsessed with the streets, listening to the traffic report on the radio at home and watching the cabs in action when I'm walking around the city, empathizing when I see that it's slow, feeling proud and happy when I observe that business is good, and generally caring about something that, to most people, is meaningless. These streets got under my skin, they became a part of me that I can't imagine will ever go away, and I'm a changed person for it.

And, as tough as the adventure has been at times, I have to admit that it has been utterly worth it. Just like during any regular twelve-hour shift over these past few years, nothing really happened—and yet everything happened. I never got robbed, never delivered a baby in the backseat, never had anything *too* insane happen, but I learned a hell of a lot. It's been a crazy, stressful, fast-paced, sometimes heartbreaking, occasionally joyous ride—a completely random chain of events strung together by a car painted yellow.

I often find myself returning to the memory of a relatively uneventful night back in the spring of 2006, after nearly two years on the job, when I ended up on 57th Street behind a pack of motorcyclists enjoying the newly warm weather. They turned left down Broadway, and I followed. They stopped at the red light at 56th Street, taking up all the lanes but one. I pulled up next to them in the one free lane to their right, and upon seeing me, one of the bikers raised his fist in solidarity and called out, "You're a soldier!"

They all turned to look at me and I wearily raised my fist back in a gesture of agreement. When the light turned green, they noisily peeled out down the avenue.

As the sound of their motors drifted away, I sat still for a second. Then, smiling a little, I hit the gas and continued down Broadway looking for my next fare.

ACKNOWLEDGMENTS

So many people helped make this thing happen, and I feel lucky for knowing every single one of them. First off, I owe a huge debt of gratitude to Erin Hosier, for being on my team and for always picking up the phone; to Bruce Tracy, for his priceless input, his honesty, and his enthusiasm; and to Richard Wissak, for all his generosity and support, as well as for always looking out for me.

Special thanks to Elliott Alboher, Mohammed Labani, Diego Lopez (my Puerto Rican brother), John McDonagh, and Allen Smerkes.

To all the friends who suffered me during the writing of this book, thank you for all your ideas, your varied contributions, and especially your patience through all the times I was a stressed-out head case: Maggie Ardelt, Gabrielle Bell, Liz Brown, Inge Colsen, Rachel Corbett, Ally Krone, Kim Ann Foxman, Dave Freedenberg, Matt Giles, Tony Groutsis, Hedia Maron, Sara Marcus, Gigi Nicolas, Kris Peterson, Alicia Relles, Lauryn Siegel, Anna Sochynsky, Frank Versace, and Nick Yapor-Cox.

Big thanks to Ryan Doherty, Laura Goldin, Ashley Gratz-Collier, Libby McGuire, Brian McLendon, Patty Park, Beth Pearson, and everyone at Villard who worked on this—you guys made it seem easy.

To all the people who've read (and liked) my blog: Your encouragement, more than anything else, made this book possible.

Huge thanks (and giant tips) go out to the cabbies, dispatchers, cashiers, and mechanics at the garage, especially Bob, Danny, Gary, Harry, Jerry, John S., Lincoln, Mario, Merrill, Pedro, Tony, Walter, Wayne, Sam, Stanley, and all the other hardworking guys at the garage with whom I've passed countless afternoons waiting for the day drivers to roll in.

Major love and gratitude to Janice Erlbaum, Meghan Folsom, Joshua Lyon, and Sharon Thomashow, all of whose advice, encouragement, reassurance, and friendship mean so much to me.

An extra-special, boldfaced, italicized, underlined, twenty-point-font thank-you to my best friend, Ariel Schrag, for putting in all those hours and for putting up with all my crap.

And, of course, a giant thank-you to my family, without whose unconditional love and support (albeit reluctant at first) none of this could have happened: Jen and Jeff; Dad and Arleen; Mom and Reno; and my grandma Gertrude, in whose apartment I wrote the first few pages of this book and then, a year later, wrote this last one.

PHOTO: © MEGHAN FOLSOM

MELISSA PLAUT was born in 1975 and grew up in the suburbs of New York City. After college, she held a series of office jobs until, at the age of twenty-nine, she began driving a yellow cab. A year later she started writing "New York Hack," a blog (http://newyorkhack.blogspot.com) about her experiences behind the wheel. Within a few months, the blog was receiving several thousand hits a day. She lives in Brooklyn.

4259